KNOW YOUR SPIRITUAL GIFTS

The Rev. Dr Mark Stibbe gained a senior scholarship at Trinity College Cambridge, where he studied English and was awarded a double first.

After a spell teaching, he began training for the ordained ministry in the Church of England, and studied for a second degree in Theology at St John's Nottingham. In 1989 he completed a PhD on John's Gospel.

Formerly vicar of St Mark's Grenoside in Sheffield, and Lecturer in the Department of Biblical Studies at the University of Sheffield, he is now Vicar of St Andrew's, Chorleywood. A leading charismatic theologian, he is a popular writer and speaker at home and abroad.

He is married to Alie and they have four children.

Know Your Spiritual Gifts

PRACTISING THE PRESENTS OF GOD

Mark Stibbe

GRAND RAPIDS, MICHIGAN 49530 USA

ZONDERVAN™

Know Your Spiritual Gifts
Copyright © 1997, 2000 Mark Stibbe

First published in Great Britain in 1997 by Marshall Pickering
This edition published 2004 by Zondervan

Mark Stibbe asserts the moral right to be identified as the author of this work

A catalogue record for this book is available from the British Library
ISBN 0-551-03243-X

Printed in the United States of America

04 05 06 07 08 09 10 \❖ DC\ 10 9 8 7 6 5 4 3 2

To Sam
This book is dedicated to our fourth child
Samuel Christopher (Born 22 June 1996)

Contents

Foreword

Recently I was in Finland with a team for a weekend of preaching and ministering in the power of the Spirit. On the Saturday afternoon we held a workshop on the gifts of the Holy Spirit, focusing specifically on prophecy and healing. We began the session with some basic biblical teaching, explaining that the gifts of the Spirit have not ceased and that the people of God can prophesy and minister healing today. We went on to explain that there is often a very close connection between these two gifts; that often we receive prophetic revelation about people with various illnesses (and indeed the Father's desire to heal those people) before praying for them in Jesus' name.

There followed a time in which my team members shared powerful and encouraging stories from their own experience. These stories were all on the same theme, 'discerning God's will prophetically, and then ministering in response to that using the gifts of healing and miraculous works'. We then encouraged the 500 or so conference delegates to wait on the Lord as we asked the Father for his kingdom rule to come upon the conference. There followed a period of silence as we listened attentively for the leading of the Spirit – for impressions, sensations, Scriptures, words, pictures and even visions, that would indicate what the Father wanted to do in our midst.

After a while in silence I asked the people if they sensed whether there were any conditions that the Lord wanted to heal. One of our team members spoke out immediately, saying something like this:

> I sense that there may be someone here with a problem with their right foot. They have broken it not long ago and it hasn't healed properly. I am fairly confident that the Lord wants to heal it today!

I asked everyone in the hall whether that applied to them. There was no response. I asked again. There was no response. I asked one final time. A young man (about 21 years old) very gingerly put his hand up. He was in fact the sound operator for the conference and had felt that because he was not a paying delegate a word like this could not apply to him! He had therefore been reluctant even to raise his hand.

Tentatively he walked forward and I interviewed him. He told us his name was Peter. He said that he had always been extremely fit and had been a fanatical runner. He also told us that he was not from Finland but from the Czech Republic. He went on to share how the previous year he had broken his right foot in three places and that the Finnish hospitals had refused him treatment because he had not been insured properly. He then had an agonizing trip by train back to the Czech Republic where the medics did a very unsatisfactory job, involving holding the broken pieces of his foot together with three pins. He was told he would never run again. He had tried once, run 12 metres, and had to rest for three days afterwards, exhausted and in great pain. However, he had come to the conference not only to do a job at the sound desk but also because his mother had received a prophetic word from the Lord that he had to go because he was going to be healed. (Thank the Lord for mothers like that!)

After hearing Peter's story, I asked a small team of Finnish people to come forward and pray with Peter. I then proceeded to ask for other words while Peter was receiving prayer.

A little later, the session was about to end. I called Peter forward and asked him if he felt any different, but he said no. People were clearly a little disappointed, but I had told everyone at the start of the session that not everyone receives healing when we pray for them, but everyone does receive a blessing. Nevertheless, I sensed a surge of faith (another gift of the Spirit) and prayed for him publicly, repeating a version of the promise of Isaiah 40:30–31, saying, 'You shall run and not grow weary!'

That evening, the next session was about to begin when Peter came up to me and asked if he could share a testimony. I asked him why he wanted to do this when nothing seemed to have happened. He replied that he had been healed. I asked him how he knew. He replied that he had just gone for a run and not stopped for twelve minutes. He felt absolutely fine. He had removed the bandages from his foot and the scars had gone.

Further discussion uncovered something even more interesting. Evidently the breakthrough had begun while the team of Finnish believers were praying for him. The conference pastor's wife had asked Peter for his forgiveness, on behalf of the Finnish people, for refusing to treat his injuries. When Peter had given his forgiveness, the healing had begun. It was a truly memorable thing that evening to watch Peter, after giving his testimony on the stage, jumping off the platform and running like an Olympic sprinter back to the sound desk!

I tell this story simply because I am certain that the gifts of the Spirit are still available, relevant and immensely powerful today. The evidence of both Scripture and experience is overwhelming on this score. I am convinced more than ever – more than before I first wrote *Know Your Spiritual Gifts* – that believers are greatly impoverished if they are ignorant of the gifts, and not only that, they are seriously limited from being a people through whom the kingdom of God can advance.

For that reason I put a very high value on teaching, training and releasing people to receive the spiritual gifts, and then to give those gifts away by using them to bless others. Furthermore, I am stressing more and more that many of these gifts – particularly prophecy, healing and miracles – are intended to bless not just believers but also those outside the church.

This came home to me forcibly last month when I took a team to Denmark. By far the most encouraging thing that happened to us did not occur in the conference among the believers but on the outward bound plane journey among unbelievers! We discovered that one of the flight attendants had a serious problem with her legs that was debilitating her in many areas of her life. Even though she was not a Christian, I asked if we could pray for her when the plane landed. She said yes, and when several of us prayed the power of God clearly came upon her. We asked her what was happening. She said she felt heat in her legs and that she was also feeling extremely emotional (in fact she was crying while she spoke).

Another flight attendant, walking by, asked me if we were praying for healing for her friend. I said we were and I asked if she was a Christian. She said no, stating that she used to be very cynical about Christianity. I asked why she said 'used to be'. She then went on to tell me that three weeks before she had been so badly afflicted with a neck problem that she had been unable to work. A Christian friend of hers had prayed for her neck with the laying on of hands and she had been instantly healed. I asked her if she was a cynic now. She said no!

Now I cannot report whether the first flight attendant was healed, or whether either of these two people came to know the Lord. I am afraid that I cannot conclude this story with a resounding, triumphant resolution. But what I can say is this: the gifts of the Holy Spirit proved indispensable for our witness to these and other unbelievers on the aircraft, and that through the healing gifts in particular two people moved a few stages closer to that point where they could confess Jesus as their Lord and Saviour.

So it is with a lot of genuine enthusiasm that I write the foreword to this new edition of *Know Your Spiritual Gifts*. I do believe very profoundly that God speaks and acts today, and that the spiritual gifts are essential if we are to cooperate with the Lord in doing his work effectively in both the church and the world.

So may the Lord richly bless you not only as you read about the gifts but also as you practise the 'presents' of God!

Mark Stibbe
February 2000

Introduction

When I was a young Christian, somebody shared a story about an auction. One day, a group of people gathered in a shop for the sale of some antiques. The auctioneer brought out an old, dusty violin. He told the audience that it was a rare Stradivarius and that it was worth a great deal of money. No one, however, was impressed; only one bid for five pounds was offered. Meanwhile a man had entered the shop from the street. He was very tall and thin, and wore a velvet coat. He walked to the front of the shop, picked up the violin, and dusted it. He then held it to his ear and reached for the bow. As he did so, a murmur went round the room, 'Paganini'. For the next few minutes, the great musician held everyone spellbound with the most exquisite virtuoso performance. Then he stopped. As he did so, the people started clamouring for the violin: fifty, sixty, seventy, eighty, ninety pounds. Eventually the violin was sold to Paganini himself for one hundred pounds, and that evening he held a vast audience of thousands in rapt attention as he played the dirty, dusty violin once again.

I have always found this a moving illustration of the importance of 'the Master's touch'. Every one of us is like that dusty violin; we are quite ordinary people, with very little to suggest any great worth in the world's eyes. Yet in God's eyes we are as valuable as a Stradivarius. In God's eyes we have been fearfully and wonderfully made, and we have been created to bring blessing to others. How, then, can we fulfil our God-given purpose and potential? The Bible reveals that it is only when Jesus Christ takes hold of our lives and cleans us up that we can start to live as God wants us to live. Jesus Christ is the one who came to erase our sins, and he has done that through his death on the cross. Jesus Christ is the one who offers us the chance to receive cleansing from the dirt of our past, and to start life all over again. Jesus Christ is in the business of giving ordinary people an extraordinary purpose. He is committed to giving insignificant people a sense of God-given significance. Like the story of Paganini, the important thing is to let the Master, Jesus Christ, take hold of our lives. Then the melody of God's creativity can come forth from our lives. Then we can seize our destiny in Christ, and our potential can truly be realized.

This, then, is one of the main reasons why I have written this book. My concern is for people to appreciate that God wants to take us, equip us and use us, for the honour of his name and for the enrichment of his Church. God is a generous Father who has gifts for all his people. The word translated gift in the New Testament is the Greek word *charisma*. As we will see in a few moments, this word is best translated as 'grace-gift'. But in modern Greek, the word *charisma* means a birthday present. The cover of this book reflects this very colourfully, with its portrayal of nine presents beautifully wrapped up, all waiting to be opened. That, for me, is a perfect picture of what awaits the reader of this book. God has at least one present or gift for you and me. It is our responsibility to find which presents have our name on them, to unwrap them, and then to enjoy using them in bringing pleasure to the Father in heaven. Our purpose, in short, is to practise the presents of God.

The Importance of the Gifts

What, then, are the gifts which God wants to give to his children? There are a number of places in the New Testament where specific gifts are mentioned. In this book I want to focus on the *charismata* or grace-gifts listed in 1 Corinthians 12:8–10. Here Paul mentions nine specific gifts:

the word of wisdom
the word of knowledge
faith
gifts of healing
miraculous powers
prophecy
discernings of spirits
speaking in different kinds of tongues
the interpretation of tongues

There are two reasons why I want to concentrate on this ninefold manifestation in 1 Corinthians 12:8–10. The first has to do with the fact that there has, in recent years, been a tremendous move of the Holy Spirit in the area of biblical scholarship. Since 1990, God has raised up many Pentecostal and Charismatic Bible scholars, and these men and women have been providing important contributions to our understanding of renewal theology.[1] One of the major blessings of this movement has been the appearance of many articles and several books on the gifts of the Holy Spirit. Part of the motivation for this scholarship has been the recognition that much of our understanding of the spiritual gifts has been dictated by experience rather than by exegesis. Today, however, there is a growing consensus that we need to begin our reflection on the gifts of the Spirit by discovering what Paul meant by these manifestations within the context of 1 Corinthians. It is one of my purposes in this book to provide something of a bridge between the academy and the Church, and to help people to understand the gifts in a fuller way. In that respect, my title – *Know Your Spiritual Gifts* – emphasizes the verb 'know'. We need to appreciate the complexity and the beauty of the gifts which God has given us. We need to 'know' them better.

A second reason for writing a book on the gifts of the Spirit has to do with certain emphases in contemporary Charismatic spirituality. Since 1994, there has been a noticeable tendency to talk about various phenomena as 'manifestations of the Holy Spirit'. Laughing, weeping, falling over, roaring and other actions are all described as 'manifestations of the Spirit'. Even though I believe most of these things are physical and emotional responses to God's potent presence, I also believe that it is dangerous to call them manifestations of the Spirit. The phrase 'manifestation of the Spirit' is used in 1 Corinthians 12:7 to describe the *charismata* which follow: word of wisdom, word of knowledge, faith, healings, miraculous works, prophecy, discernings of spirits, different kinds of tongues, interpretation of tongues. Once we start adding other things to that list we not only run the risk of adding to Scripture, we also start to prefer exotic phenomena to the gifts of grace. As David du Plessis once put it:

> Let me say right here that I consider it heresy to speak of shaking, trembling, falling, dancing, clapping, shouting, and such actions as manifestations of the Holy Spirit. These are purely human reactions to the power of the Holy Spirit … There are far too many Christians who are satisfied with such emotional reactions and thus do not seek to grow in grace and become channels through whom the Holy Spirit may manifest his gifts for the edification of the Church.[2]

That was written in 1963, but it is still relevant today. One of the purposes of this book is to encourage people not to neglect the *charismata* in favour of physical and emotional reactions to the presence of the Holy Spirit.

The Nature of the Gifts

Where do the spiritual gifts come from? Paul writes that the source of the gifts is in the Trinitarian God. That is to say, they all derive from the Father, the Son and the Holy Spirit. The clearest evidence of this is in 1 Corinthians 12:4-6, where Paul says,

> There are different kinds of gifts, but the same Spirit;
> There are different kinds of service, but the same Lord;
> There are different kinds of working, but the same God
> works all of them in all men.

Paul states that the gifts are from the Spirit, the Lord, and from God. The Spirit refers to the Holy Spirit. The 'Lord' (*kurios* in Greek) refers to Jesus, whom every true believer acknowledges as 'Lord' (12:3). The word God refers to God the Father. Here, then, is the decisive argument against those who see the gifts of the Spirit purely in terms of natural talents. The gifts of the Spirit derive from the tri-une God – the God who is Father, Son and Holy Spirit. They originate in the Father, are given by the Son, and are mediated in the power of the Holy Spirit. No one can therefore boast of their gifts because they are first and foremost concrete expressions of God's grace. This much is indicated by the word which Paul coins to describe these gifts – *charisma* in the singular, *charismata* in the plural. This word derives from the root word *charis* meaning 'grace'. Grace, in turn, is the love and favour which God showers upon unde-serving sinners like you and me. By using the word *charismata* for the gifts of the Spirit, Paul is making a concerted effort to prevent people from seeing the source of the gifts in terms of natural abilities alone. He wants us to understand that the gifts are unmerited endowments not personal achievements. They are 'God's birthday presents', given to every new-born believer, by the Exalted Christ.

Paul uses a number of words to describe the nature of the gifts given by the Spirit. In the passage just quoted, he says that there are different 'gifts' but the same Spirit, different kinds of 'service', but the same Lord, and different kinds of 'working' but the same God. The first word which Paul uses is *charismata*, translated as 'gifts'. Prior to the writings of Paul, this word is only used twice in the whole of the Greek translation of the Old Testament (known as the Septuagint, or LXX for short). On both occasions it is used in the apocryphal book of Ecclesiasticus (at 7:33 and 38:30). On the first occasion there is an element of doubt about whether *charisma* is actually used. Some manuscripts have *charisma* while others have *charis*. In the second case, however, there is a greater element of certainty. In Ecclesiasticus 38:30, the word *charisma* is used to denote 'a lovely work'. Though it would be wrong to read too much into this translation, it is nevertheless attractive to think of the gifts of the Holy Spirit as 'lovely works', especially when they are used by the believer in a sensitive way.

There is therefore some evidence to suggest that Paul uses the word *charisma* in a way which is distinctively his own. This word occurs 17 times in the New Testament and, with the exception of 1 Peter 4:10, all the references are to be found in Paul's letters. Paul uses this word in two ways, one general, the other specific. In the general sense, the word refers to God's grace, specifically to the saving work of Jesus Christ. Thus Paul writes,

> The free gift (*charisma*) of God is eternal life in
> Christ Jesus.   (Romans 6:23)

Here *charisma* clearly refers to something far broader than just a grace-gift for Christian ministry. In other instances, however, Paul uses the word in a far more specific sense, to refer to the special abilities which God gives to every member of the Body of Christ. Thus Paul writes,

> Each man has his own grace-gift (*charisma*) from God.
>   (1 Corinthians 7:7)

Here the word refers to particular gifts given by the Holy Spirit to the believer. The overall picture therefore looks like this:

CHARISMA (general sense)
Romans 5:15
Romans 5:16
Romans 6:23
Romans 11:29

CHARISMA (specific sense)
Romans 1:11
Romans 12:6
1 Corinthians 1:7
1 Corinthians 7:7
1 Corinthians 12:4
1 Corinthians 12:9
1 Corinthians 12:28
1 Corinthians 12:30
1 Corinthians 12:31

1 Timothy 4:14
2 Timothy 1:6

This survey shows that Paul uses *charisma* in the general sense quite sparingly, whereas he uses it in the specific sense more frequently.

The word *charisma* is therefore Paul's principal way of describing what in common parlance are described as the 'spiritual gifts'. Two other words he uses are 'works of service' (*diakoniai*, from which we get the word 'deacon', meaning a 'servant of God') and 'workings' (*energemata*, from which we get the word 'energy'). Paul uses the first when he writes that there are different kinds of *service* but the same Lord. He uses the second when he writes that there are different kinds of *working*, but the same God (1 Corinthians 12:5–6). The first word is important because it highlights the fact that the spiritual gifts are given so that we can serve others in the Body of Christ; they are given to be given away. The second word is important because it suggests that every grace-gift is an example of God's 'energy' or power at work in our lives.

Paul's teaching in 1 Corinthians 12:4–6 therefore reveals three things about the nature of the Spirit's gifts. The word *charismata*, first of all, points to their origin. It reveals that they are first and foremost gifts of God's grace. They are tokens of God's undeserved love. The word *diakoniai*, secondly, suggests their purpose. They are gifts given for serving God and for serving others. They are not to be held and hoarded as personal blessings. They are given in order that we may be a blessing to others. The word *energemata*, thirdly, reveals their power. They are not natural abilities which we use in our human strength. Rather, they are an expression of the power of the Holy Spirit. Indeed, Paul describes the gifts as 'manifestations' of the Spirit. The Holy Spirit is like an electric current: invisible, yet real. The gifts of the Spirit are like footlights illuminated by this current; they are a manifestation of the power at work in them. The one on whom these lights are focused, furthermore, is the Lord Jesus Christ, who should always stand centre-stage in the Church. The gifts of the Spirit are therefore grace-gifts, works of service, spiritual 'workings', and manifestations of the Spirit.

The Purpose of the Gifts

Why does God give these gifts to his Church? The simple answer to that is found in the phrase 'for the common good', used in 1 Corinthians 12:7: 'Now to each one the manifestation of the Spirit is given *for the common good*.' The purpose of the grace-gifts of the Spirit is quite simply 'for the good of the Church'. This becomes very clear when Paul talks about the gift of prophecy. In 1 Corinthians 14:4 he writes, 'he who prophesies edifies the Church.' The word 'edifies' is interesting. In Greek it is, 'speaking edification'. 'Edification' is an architectural term used for building houses (*oikodome*). Paul uses this metaphor in the context of prophecy because, like all the gifts, its purpose is to build up the house of God, not to tear it down. Its purpose is to strengthen not to weaken the Church.

Of course, the great danger with the gifts of the Spirit, especially the more spectacular ones such as tongues, healing and prophecy, is that they become a focus of division rather than of unity. It seems that this is precisely what was going on in the Corinthian church. From Paul's first letter we can see that a super-spiritual élite was emerging, whose fault was an over-emphasis on the more extraordinary and sensational gifts. They were claiming to be more spiritual than those who did not receive revelation from God, who did not speak out inspired utterances, and who did not perform dramatic miracles. Paul chastises these people by reminding them that every one in the Body of Christ is given gifts of the Spirit, that these gifts are the result of God's grace not human achievement, and that they are for the common good, not for personal advancement. In other words, he underlines the purpose of the gifts, which is to serve the community of faith rather than our own ends.

It is for this reason that Paul speaks about the gifts of the Spirit in connection with his picture of the Church as the Body of Christ. In Romans 12:4–5, he introduces his list of the gifts with the following remark:

> Just as each one of us has one body with many members, and these members do not all have the same function, so in Christ we who are many form one body, and each member belongs to the others.

Paul's strategy is therefore to talk about the gifts of the Spirit in a corporate rather than an individualistic way. He will not talk about an individual receiving and using a gift for their own sake. But he will talk about an individual receiving a gift or gifts for the benefit of the body of the Church. This is precisely what happens in 1 Corinthians 12. The first section of the chapter deals with the gifts of the Spirit (vv. 1–11), the second with the Church as the Body of Christ (vv. 12–26), the third with the gifts of the Spirit again (vv. 27–31).

A: 12:1–11: The Gifts of the Spirit
B: 12:12–26: The Church as the Body of Christ
A: 12:27–31: The Gifts of the Spirit

Paul therefore sandwiches his discussion of the spiritual gifts around a passage describing the Church as Christ's body. Again, the emphasis is upon the use of the gifts for the sake of the community rather than for the individual. The church where the gifts are openly welcomed and responsibly handled is a healthy, a dynamic and a living church. As one Bible scholar has put it:

Let it be firmly said that the Church cannot be fully or freely the Church without the presence and operation of the gifts of the Holy Spirit. What is depicted therefore in 1 Corinthians – and recurring in our day – is in no sense a peripheral matter but is crucial to the life of the Church. For the resurgence of the *charismata* of the Holy Spirit signals the Church's recovery of its spiritual roots and its emergence in the twentieth century with fresh power and vitality.[3]

The Employment of the Gifts

It is because of this corporate purpose for the gifts that Paul stresses the need for 'love' in the use of the gifts. As has often been pointed out, Paul does this by constructing his argument in chapters 12–14 in this way:

    A: 1 Corinthians 12: The Gifts of the Spirit
    B: 1 Corinthians 13: A Celebration of Love
    A: 1 Corinthians 14: The Gifts of the Spirit

No one can miss the importance of the central passage about love in this design. In 1 Corinthians 13, Paul stresses the need for *agape*, for self-sacrificial love, if the gifts are to be employed responsibly and constructively. Indeed, in this chapter alone the word *agape* is used nine times. In Romans 12:1–8, the same note of 'sacrificial love' is struck when Paul comes to discuss the gifts of the Spirit. Before he has even mentioned any of the gifts, he writes:

> Therefore, I urge you, brothers, in view of God's mercy, to offer your
> bodies as living sacrifices, holy and pleasing to God – this is your spir-
> itual act of worship.

Here again Paul emphasizes the need to be full of *agape* love for both God and for others if the gifts are to be a blessing to the Church. Only those who are prepared to walk in the Calvary love of God can rightly handle the blessings of Pentecost. If we are to use the gifts of the Spirit in a constructive and responsible manner, we must therefore remember what Paul describes as the 'excellent way of love'. We must be more preoccupied with the power of love than with the love of power. With that in mind, it is good to pray the beautiful prayer of Yves Congar:

> May it please the Spirit at certain times and in certain places to release
> a veritable Niagara of charisms! This is a gift that fills us with praise
> and makes us sing of God's marvels. But all the charisms exist only for
> charity [love], which is their summit and their only criterion ... there
> is nothing beyond love.[4]

Amen to that!

The Pursuit of the Gifts

How, then, do we become a 'gifted' person? How do we become a 'charismatic' in the root sense of the word? The most important thing to say at this point is this: that it is impossible to receive the gifts of the Spirit until we have received the gift of the Holy Spirit. We receive the gift of the Spirit when we are initiated into the kingdom of God. This process of initiation involves repentance of sin, faith in Jesus Christ, baptism in water, and baptism in the Holy Spirit. The New Testament writers believe that we cannot become fully function-ing members of the Body of Christ until we have experienced these aspects of effective and complete initiation. Paul says in 1 Corinthians 12:13 that we were all baptized by one Spirit into one body (i.e. the Church). It stands to reason, therefore, that we cannot operate in the gifts of the Spirit until we have been baptized in the Holy Spirit. Receiving the Holy Spirit at our conversion-initiation is the way in to the reception and the release of the gifts. As Rod Williams has put it:

> The charismatic renewal of our day is in basic accord with the Corinthian situation. The background for the believers' claims to the operation of the gifts of the Holy Spirit is their experience of the out-pouring of the Spirit. At some time, in some situation, there has been a distinctive – even 'saturating' – experience of the Holy Spirit's pres-ence and power. This has been, it is claimed, the dynamic source of all the spiritual gifts that have followed.[5]

Baptism in the Holy Spirit is the unavoidable prerequisite of authentic, charismatic Christianity.

If it is important to be baptized in the Holy Spirit, it is also impor-tant to believe that all the gifts of the Holy Spirit are available today. In contemporary Christianity there are, broadly speaking, three views on the gifts of the Spirit. There is the liberal view which says that the spiritual gifts, such as miraculous works, did not really happen in the time of the apostles, and they do not really happen today. There is the conservative view, which says that they did happen in the time of the apostles, but they do not happen today. Then there is the Pentecostal and Charismatic view which says that they did happen in the time of the apostles, and they do happen in today's Church. If we are to find and use our spiritual gifts then it is imperative that we believe that *all* the gifts are available today. So what is the evidence that they are still available? The most important clue is in 1 Corinthians 13, Paul's eulogy of love. There he states that prophecy, tongues and knowledge will cease 'when perfection comes' (13:8–10). What does Paul mean? The following interpretations have been offered.

1 The gifts of the Spirit are to be in operation until the closing of the canon. 'When perfection comes' refers to the completion of the canon of Scripture. Since that happened long ago, the gifts are no longer necessary.

2 The gifts of the Spirit are to be in operation until the Church gains maturity. Since the Church has gained maturity, the gifts are no longer necessary. C. S. Lewis said that 'miracles are for beginners'. This goes for all the gifts. They are for babes not adults.

3 The gifts of the Spirit are to be in operation until Jesus Christ returns. In this interpretation, 'when perfection comes' refers to the *parousia* or return of Christ. Since he has not returned, the gifts are still available.[6]

I am a firm believer in accepting the plain sense of Scripture where Scripture seems to me to be 'plain' in its 'sense'! The word translated 'perfection' is *teleios* in Greek. The most obvious translation of this word is 'the end' – referring, of course, to the end of history. When Paul says that gifts such as prophecy, knowledge and tongues will cease 'when the end comes', he is basically saying the following:

When the end of history arrives, and Jesus Christ returns, then we will find that the gifts of the Holy Spirit such as tongues, knowledge and prophecy, will cease. They will cease because they are no longer necessary in the new heaven and the new earth. Why? Because the gifts are imperfect means of knowing God. When the end comes, however, our ability to know the Lord will be perfect. Imperfect means of knowing him will cease and pass away.

Thus, Paul teaches that the gifts of the Spirit are available today. They are the means by which the exalted Christ equips the Church until the *eschaton*, until the end of the age. There is no hint anywhere in the New Testament that these gifts were only designed for the apostolic era (i.e. the first century AD). As Siegfried Schatzmann has put it, in his book *A Pauline Theology of Charismata*:

> Nothing in the text of 1 Corinthians 13, or in any other Pauline passage concerned with charismatic endowment, permits the conclusion that certain gifts of the Spirit were to function for a limited initial period only.[7]

Paul's teaching is that the gifts of the Spirit are essential for the 'inbetween times' – for the time between the 'already' of Jesus' first coming, and the 'not yet' of Jesus' *parousia* or return. Even church history bears this out. There are many instances of the gifts being used after the first century. As we shall see in our chapter on 'the gift of miraculous works', church history reveals that there has been plenty of examples of the *charismata* over the last two thousand years. This is what Irenaeus wrote in the second century:

> For some drive out demons with certainty and truth, so that often those who have themselves been cleansed from evil spirits believe and are in the Church, and some have foreknowledge of things to be, and visions and prophetic speech, and others cure the sick by the laying on of hands and make them whole, and even as we have said, the dead have been raised and remained with us for many years. And why should I say more? It is not possible to tell the number of the gifts which the Church throughout the whole world, having received them from God in the name of Jesus Christ, who was crucified under Pontius Pilate, uses each day for the benefit of the heathen, deceiving none, and making profit from none. For as it received freely from God, it ministers also freely.[8]

If we are to become 'charismatic' in the Pauline sense of the word, we must not only be baptized in the Holy Spirit, we must also believe that the grace-gifts of the Spirit are available for us until the end of all things occurs. Faith is therefore vital. There must be faith in the general sense outlined above – faith that the gifts are for now, not just for the first century. There must be faith in the specific sense, that God has gifts specifically for us to discover and to use. It is our duty to be informed about the gifts (1 Corinthians 12:1), to desire the gifts (1 Corinthians 14:1), to use the gifts (1 Peter 4:10) and, when necessary, to rekindle the gifts (2 Timothy 1:6). In this process, ongoing faith is indispensable.

The Extent of the Gifts

All this leads us to two related questions. The first one concerns how many spiritual gifts there are altogether, the second has to do with the number which a Christian can expect to receive. In answer to the first question, it is important to remember that the lists of the spiritual gifts in the New Testament are not exhaustive. In Romans 12 there are gifts which are mentioned in 1 Corinthians 12. But there are also some which are not. Furthermore, in 1 Corinthians 7:7, Paul implies that celibacy or sexual continency is a *charisma*. Yet he does not mention this charism in either of his lists in 1 Corinthians 12 or Romans 12. This suggests that there is a wide variety of gifts.

Does this mean that every Christian is supposed to have all the gifts? The answer to that is 'no'. Paul asks a number of rhetorical questions at the end of 1 Corinthians 12 which all begin with the Greek word *me* – a word which tells us that the answer in each case is supposed to be 'no'.

Are all apostles? No.
Are all prophets? No.
Are all teachers? No.
Do all work miracles? No.
Do all have gifts of healing? No.
Do all speak in tongues? No.
Do all interpret? No.
(1 Corinthians 12:29–30)

For Paul, then, it is not God's intention for a Christian to be 'omni-charismatic' – to have all the spiritual gifts. Far from it! He says, 'to *each one* the manifestation of the Spirit is given' (12:7). He then uses the two words *hetero* and *allo* (both meaning 'another') to drive the point home:

to one a word of wisdom
to another (*allo*) a word of knowledge
to another (*hetero*) faith
to another (*allo*) gifts of healing
to another (*allo*) works of power
to another (*allo*) prophecy
to another (*allo*) distinguishing between spirits
to another (*hetero*) kinds of tongues
to another (*allo*) interpretation of tongues.
(1 Corinthians 12:8–10)

These verses indicate that every Christian has a particular manifestation of the Spirit. That manifestation is described by Paul as a 'grace-gift' given by the Holy Spirit as he determines (1 Corinthians 12:11). This does not mean that we are destined to receive only one gift during the course of our Christian lives. The truth of the matter is this: that we are all supposed to have the gift of prophecy (1 Corinthians 14:31), and Paul desires that every one of us should speak in tongues. On top of those gifts, we will very likely have a primary gift which is often accompanied by other relevant and related gifts. For example, those who know me say that my primary gift is teaching. On some occasions God combines this gift with prophecy. Furthermore, in teaching from the Word, God may, from time to time, give me a word of wisdom or a word of knowledge. On other occasions he may give me a gift of faith that a group of people are going to respond in a particular way. He may likewise choose to give me discernment about the 'spirits' present in a meeting where I have to teach. All sorts of permutations are therefore possible with the gifts. The important thing to recognize is that no one has all the gifts. We all have some, and the gifts we do have are determined by the Holy Spirit, according to the needs around us.

To summarize: the extent of the gifts is probably more than what Scripture specifically describes. However, in this book I am not going to run the risk of adding to Scripture by including special abilities or callings which are not explicitly referred to as *charismata* in the New Testament. I shall stick to those which are mentioned in 1 Corinthians 12:8–10. Furthermore, I believe that every disciple of Christ has been given a primary grace-gift by the Holy Spirit. To each one is given a special manifestation of the Spirit which he or she must identify, nurture and use. Over the course of time, if that person is faithful and fruitful in the use of that gift, then that may be recognized by the leadership of a church, and may subsequently be turned into a ministry. That, of course, will depend not only on the person's obedience but also the situation of the church in question. The key thing in the first place is to know your spiritual gifts.

God's Birthday Presents

That brings me back to the front cover, and to the picture of the beautifully wrapped presents. There is a tendency in some people to say that the *charismata* are not for today. Those people are like children who never expect any kind of gift from their fathers. On their birthday, they do not believe that there is a gift waiting to be opened and enjoyed. If you are one of those, I would like to encourage you to consider the claims of this book, and to acknowledge that God is a Father who gives good gifts to his children, and who gives them today (Luke 11:13).

There are others who do acknowledge the gift that the Father has given to them, but they are more preoccupied with the gift than the Giver. They are like children who revel in the present but neglect to give thanks to the parent who cared enough to give it to them in the first place. If you are one of those, then I would like to encourage you to put your focus once more on the Lord rather than on the anointing which he may, by grace, have given you. It is so important to remember the modesty of the Spirit; his delight is in pointing to the Father and to the Son, not to himself.

Then there are those who have received a gift but are not content with it. They want a more spectacular anointing, but instead they have been given something less visible and more ordinary. These people are like children who see what their brother or their sister has received, and then set about comparing and complaining. If you are one of those, I would like to encourage you to learn contentment. Be grateful for what God has given you. If it is one of the less spectacular gifts, remember that it is still a gift and that your part in the Body is as essential as the one played by the worker of miracles, the well-known speaker, or the authentic prophet. Remember also that God may call you from waiting on tables to working miracles and preaching the Gospel, as he did with Stephen (see Acts 6–7). So be faithful in the little tasks, and do not forget to ask for the gift of prophecy!

The chapters which follow are designed to help you identify which gift has your name on it, to unwrap that gift, and to start using and enjoying it to the glory of God. My earnest prayer is that everyone who reads this book will feel included not excluded, and that all will be enabled to 'practise the presents of God'. Pentecost inaugurated a wonderful democracy of the Holy Spirit. As one Orthodox hymn writer once put it:

> The Holy Spirit provides all,
> overflows with prophecy,
> fulfils the priesthood,
> has taught wisdom to illiterates,
> and revealed fishermen as theologians.[9]

If that is true (and we should know that it is), then there is a gift and a ministry waiting for everyone in the Body of Christ. My prayer is therefore the prayer of Yves Congar:

> May there be a better climate in our parishes and communities, a better attitude on the part of believers, a better education in faith and a better knowledge of the charisms, so that the Spirit may be more able to fill the people of God![10]

ONE

The Word of Wisdom

If you were asked to make a list of the spiritual gifts, which one would you put first and which one would you put last? If we look at Paul's list in 1 Corinthians 12, we will quickly see that he has a rather topsy-turvy understanding of charismatic priorities – at least from a worldly point of view. His list is in the following order:

1   The word of wisdom
2   The word of knowledge
3   Faith
4   Gifts of healing
5   Miraculous works
6   Prophecy
7   Discernings of spirits
8   Tongues
9   Interpretation of tongues

Paul puts tongues and interpretation last on his list. That is the exact opposite of what you might expect, given the emphasis placed on tongue-speaking in some churches. Indeed, you may know the joke concerning the motto of the unbalanced Christian:

These three remain – faith, hope and love;
but the greatest of these is tongues!

We might have been tempted to put tongues first and wisdom last! Paul does the exact opposite. Why? Because he recognizes that tongues must not be over-valued and wisdom must not be under-valued. Indeed, there are few contexts in which wisdom is more urgently required than in our theology and practice of the spiritual gifts. Maybe it is for this reason that Paul puts the word of wisdom first on his list.

The Nature of the Gift

In popular Charismatic teaching, 'the word of wisdom' is understood as 'an inspired application of a word of knowledge'. The word of knowledge is defined as a supernatural insight into hidden facets of a person or a situation. The word of wisdom is understood as the charismatic application of this knowledge. Thus Peter Wagner, author of a well-known and influential book entitled *Your Spiritual Gifts Can Help Your Church Grow*, in many ways typifies this popular understanding of these two gifts. He defines 'the word of wisdom' as

the special ability that God gives to certain members of the Body of Christ to know the mind of the Holy Spirit in such a way as to receive insight into how given knowledge may best be applied to specific situations ...[1]

This understanding of wisdom has now entered into the common vocabulary of Charismatic churches. The example which is often cited from Scripture is the encounter between Jesus and the Samaritan woman in John 4. Jesus receives a 'word of knowledge' about the woman – that she has been married to five men, and is living *de facto* with a sixth. He then exercises the 'word of wisdom' by teaching her about worshipping God. Today this passage is regarded as the *locus classicus* – that is, the authoritative passage – for discussing 'the word of wisdom', and it is not, to my knowledge, ever questioned.

Is this definition of the gift of wisdom correct? If we begin by asking what Paul meant by 'the word of wisdom', we shall see that he intended something more than just an impression or a thought or a vision or the direct audible voice of the Holy Spirit from God about HOW to deal with a situation.[2]

The phrase 'word of wisdom' is *logos sophias* in the Greek. The word (*logos*) can be translated as 'message' or 'utterance', and this indicates that Paul saw the gift as something manifested through inspired speech. When we ask what kind of speech Paul was referring to, the answer is *sophia*, referring to a divine rather than a purely intellectual wisdom. In a very general sense, this particular gift should be defined as an act of communication involving two processes. First of all, it needs to be understood as a message communicated by the Holy Spirit to a believer. I define that as *a sudden insight given by the Holy Spirit concerning God's wisdom*. At a second level we need to talk in terms of the communication of this message by the one who receives it. I define this aspect as *the special ability on the part of the receiver to express this charismatic insight so that the Church is encouraged and edified.* Looking at it as a whole, we can therefore define the 'word of wisdom' as two gifts rolled into one: it is the gift of being able to understand and to express something of God's wisdom, in such a way that the Church is built up and strengthened.

Theological Wisdom

So far it may seem as if I am in broad agreement with the standard interpretation of the 'word of wisdom'. However, I believe that there is more to this gift than is commonly appreciated. In particular, I would like to suggest that the past antipathy of some Charismatics to theology has blinded many to the deeper and broader nature of this charismatic gift. If we look at the second chapter of 1 Corinthians, we quickly see that 'wisdom' is concerned with the great scope of what has been called 'salvation history', not just with God's purposes in the circumstances of a church or an individual. In 1 Corinthians 2, Paul sees divine 'wisdom' as something hidden for many generations, but now disclosed in the person of Jesus. In particular, God's plan concerning the atoning death of

Jesus is seen as the ultimate 'mystery' of God. Here is Eugene Petersen's paraphrase of the relevant part of that chapter:

> We, of course, have plenty of *wisdom* to pass on to you once you get your feet on firm spiritual ground, but it's not popular *wisdom*, the fashionable *wisdom* of high-priced experts that will be out-of-date in a year or so. God's *wisdom* is something mysterious that goes deep into the interior of his purposes. You don't find it lying around on the surface. It's not the latest message, but more like the oldest – what God determined as the way to bring out his best in us, long before we ever arrived on the scene. The experts of our day haven't a clue about what his eternal plan is. If they had, they wouldn't have killed the Master of the God-designed life on a cross. [Italics mine.] [3]

For Paul, then, God's wisdom is a *mysterion* – a mystery. To the finite and fallen minds of even the best philosophers, God's wisdom is opaque and hidden. The reason for this is because divine wisdom is tied up with God's secret plan of redemption! God had it in mind from the beginning of time to put into operation an international rescue plan. He saw that humanity would, in Adam, fall from grace through sin. He also saw that our desperate attempts to be reconciled to God would never work. Something from God's side rather than ours was going to be necessary. So God decided that at just the right time, he would send his only Son into the world, and allow him to be crucified as an atonement for sin. Thus, Calvary constitutes the heart of God's 'secret wisdom', God's secret purpose. There, on that blood-spattered, rain-drenched cross, sin's price was paid and salvation was made available to all. To the natural or 'unspiritual mind', this of course is nonsense. It represents utter foolishness. But to the 'spiritual person' (i.e. the one filled with the Spirit), it all makes perfect sense. With the help of the revelatory work of the Spirit we are able to understand something of God's wisdom in giving us his Son. Without the Holy Spirit we could never appreciate how an ignominious crucifixion could do away with sin. We could never grasp the fact that:

The cross is a picture of violence, yet the key to peace;
a picture of suffering, yet the key to healing;
a picture of death, yet the key to life;
a picture of utter weakness, yet the key to power;
a picture of capital punishment, yet the key to mercy and forgiveness;
a picture of vicious hatred, yet the key to love;
a picture of supreme shame, yet the Christian's supreme boast. [4]

The only way we can understand the paradoxical wisdom of the cross of Christ is through the illuminating work of the Holy Spirit. The natural mind cannot fathom the depths of God's infinite wisdom. Only the mind which is imbued with the Spirit can penetrate the depths of 'love divine'. Here is Eugene Petersen again:

The Spirit, not content to flit around on the surface, dives into the depths of God, and brings out what God planned all along. Who ever knows what you're thinking and planning except you yourself? The same with God – except that he not only knows what he's thinking, but he lets *us* in on it. [5]

So it is the Holy Spirit who gives us understanding concerning the secret wisdom of God. As Petersen translates it. 'God by his Spirit has brought it all out into the open before you'. This means that the 'word of wisdom' should be defined as *a charismatic revelation into God's secret, redemptive purposes in history*. It should be seen first and foremost as an inspired word concerning the secret heavenly wisdom behind the death of an emaciated carpenter in ancient Palestine. I think we would all agree that it takes spiritual revelation to understand a paradox of this magnitude. This is precisely Paul's point. He refuses to preach the message of the cross relying on 'wise words' (*sophias logois*, 1 Corinthians 2:4) – i.e. on philosophical eloquence. No one would understand the wisdom of God through such human effort. So Paul relies not on the wisdom of words but on 'words of wisdom'. He depends on the Holy Spirit, who gives charismatic insight into God's secret purposes, and then enables the believers to articulate those insights in a life-changing way. The 'word of wisdom' in Paul's understanding is, accordingly, a revelation of God's mysterious, general purposes for mankind.

Practical Wisdom

When Paul speaks of 'the word of wisdom', I believe he primarily means 'theological wisdom'; that is, God's general purposes in salvation history. However, biblical 'wisdom' is never confined to theology alone. In Scripture, 'wisdom' is 'practical' or 'ethical' as well. In other words, God gives wisdom to his servants when they need to know how to act or speak in difficult and perplexing situations. This is particularly obvious in the ministry of Jesus. Mark's gospel alone has several examples of Jesus ministering practical wisdom. A few obvious ones are these:

> **Mark 2:13–17.** When Jesus is eating at Levi's house, the Pharisees question why he is eating with tax collectors and sinners, and Jesus replies, 'It is not the healthy who need a doctor, but the sick'.

> **Mark 3:20–30.** When Jesus is accused of driving out demons with demonic power, he replies, 'How can Satan drive out Satan? If a kingdom is divided against itself it cannot stand.'

> **Mark 7:1–23.** When the Pharisees question Jesus about his attitude towards the purity laws, he replies: 'Nothing outside a man can make him "unclean" by going into him. Rather, it is what comes out of a man that makes him "unclean".'

> **Mark 12:13–17.** When Jesus is questioned about paying taxes to Caesar, he takes a denarius and says, 'Give to Caesar what is Caesar's and to God what is God's.'

In each of these cases, and in many others, Jesus expresses a special insight of wisdom. When the people in Jesus' local synagogue ask, 'Where does he get such wisdom from?' (Matthew 13:54), the answer is, 'he gets it from the Spirit'. Jesus' wisdom is charismatic wisdom, and, as such, is full of divine *exousia* or authority. As James Dunn has put it:

> This is not the self-confidence of massive erudition deriving from rab-
> binic schooling or proper status deriving from ceremony and ritual,
> but a powerful certainty of a direct and unmediated kind – a charis-
> matic insight in particular situations into the will of God.[6]

Perhaps the most dramatic example of Jesus' use of the gift of wisdom is in John 8:1–11. In this story a number of Pharisees and teachers of the law catch an adulteress red-handed. What they were doing spying on a woman committing adultery is, of course, an interesting question, especially when you consider how preoc-cupied they are with absolute sexual holiness! Be that as it may, they bring the poor, dishevelled and humiliated woman before Jesus because their intention is to trap him. If he shows leniency and lets her go, then they can accuse him of being lawless. The Torah, after all, commands that she be put to death by stoning. If, on the other hand, he condemns her and demands her immediate execution, then they can accuse him of being loveless. The Messi-ah, after all, should be a man of compassion. This, then, is a des-perate moral dilemma. Either way, it looks like a no-win situation for Jesus. Whatever course of action he chooses, it seems that he can be condemned for behaviour unbecoming of the Messiah of Israel.

So what does Jesus do? His immediate response is interesting. He bends down and starts writing something in the sand. We are not told what he wrote; that is not important to John, who tells the story. What is important is to recognize that Jesus is giving himself a few precious moments to listen to what the Father is saying and to receive heavenly wisdom. Having heard that wisdom, he stands upright again and addresses the crowd. The *logos sophias* which is given to him by the Holy Spirit is this:

> If anyone of you is without sin, let him be the first to throw a stone
> at her.

In one fell swoop, the tables are turned on the accusers. Having sought to trap Jesus, his opponents find themselves trapped instead. It is they who are now in a moral dilemma. If any of them throws a stone at the woman now, they can justifiably be accused of gross spiritual pride. If anyone fails to throw a stone, then that person can justifiably be said to be revealing himself as an adulterer! So they walk away, the older ones first (presumably because the older ones are wise enough to recognize true wisdom when they see it, Job 12:12).

At this point Jesus, who has stooped down again to draw in the sand, stands upright and addresses the woman. Again, he has been spending a few moments waiting on the Holy Spirit for a word of wisdom to give to the one so horribly abused and exploited before him. Here again, the need for wisdom is obvious. If Jesus fails to show her compassion, he can be accused of being loveless. If he fails to point out the need for sexual holiness, then he can once again be accused of being lawless. So Jesus begins by reassuring the woman of his affirmation and acceptance. 'Neither do I condemn you,' he says. Jesus begins with a word of compassion and mercy. But he does not end there. He tells the woman that she is to go and leave her life of sin. Having shown the forgiveness of God, he warns her not to sin again. In this way, Jesus avoids the two extremes of soft liberalism and harsh legalism. He will not exercise compassion without morality, nor will he teach morality without compassion. His whole approach to this situation is a wonderful example of how to love the sinner without neglecting God's abhorrence of sin.

Wisdom and the Spirit

Given this strong tradition concerning the charismatic wisdom of Jesus, it seems more than likely that Paul understood the 'word of wisdom' in a practical as well as a theological sense. This is further confirmed by the way in which practical words of wisdom are described in the Old Testament. For example, in the famous story of Pharaoh's dream (Genesis 41), we see this relationship between wisdom and the Spirit worked out in the life of Joseph. Pharaoh has a dream of seven skinny cows devouring seven fat cows. He turns to his own wise men and asks them for the meaning of the dream, and they are unable to interpret it for him. Pharaoh then calls for Joseph, who tells him that the dream is a warning that there will be seven years of plenty followed by seven years of scarcity. Joseph also tells Pharaoh that he should appoint someone to administrate the seven plentiful harvests in order to prepare for the seven subsequent years of great need. When Pharaoh hears this, he turns to his court advisers and applauds Joseph for being so evidently full of the 'Spirit of Elohim' (*ruach elohim*). He then looks at Joseph and tells him that there is no one as wise in all his kingdom.[7]

In this story, the Scriptures reveal the connection between *ruach* (the Holy Spirit) and *hokma* (wisdom). It is the Holy Spirit who gives wisdom to the wise and knowledge to the discerning (see Daniel 5:10–16). It is the Spirit of God, the searcher of the divine depths, who reveals the hidden things of God. No wonder, then, that the Hebrew Bible is so full of what has been called 'wisdom literature'. The pithy sayings in the Book of Proverbs and in the Book of Ecclesiastes give just some of the many examples of Spirit-inspired utterances of heavenly wisdom which we find in the Scriptures:

> Blessed is the man who finds wisdom,
>> the man who gains understanding,
> For she is more profitable than silver
>> and yields better returns than gold.
> She is more precious than rubies;
>> nothing you desire can compare with her. (Proverbs 3:13–15)

> There is a time for everything,
>> and a season for every activity under heaven;
> a time to be born and a time to die,
> a time to plant and a time to uproot,
> a time to kill and a time to heal,
> a time to tear down and a time to build,
> a time to weep and a time to laugh,
> a time to mourn and a time to dance,

a time to scatter stones and a time to gather them,
a time to embrace and a time to refrain,
a time to search and a time to give up,
a time to keep and a time to throw away,
a time to tear and a time to mend,
a time to be silent and a time to speak,
a time to love and a time to hate,
a time for war and a time for peace. (Ecclesiastes 3:1-8)

As time went by, the people of Israel began to yearn for the coming of the Messiah. They saw this Messianic figure as a person who would be endowed with the Holy Spirit and consequently full of wisdom. One example of this expectation from within the canonical Scriptures is Isaiah 11:2, a prophecy of the coming Messiah:

The Spirit of the Lord will rest on him –
    the Spirit of wisdom and of understanding,
    the Spirit of counsel and of power,
    the Spirit of knowledge and the fear of the Lord.

Here Isaiah prophesies the coming of the ideal king to reign over Israel. This king would have God's *ruach* resting on him. He would also manifest the six charismatic virtues of 'wisdom and understanding, counsel and power, knowledge and holy fear'. The gospels make it plain that this prophecy was eventually fulfilled in the person of Jesus. At Jesus' baptism, the Spirit of God descends from heaven and 'rests' upon him (John 1:32-33), conferring upon him all the virtues predicted in Isaiah 11:2. No wonder, then, that Paul can describe Jesus of Nazareth as the Wisdom and Power of God (1 Corinthians 1:24). Jesus is not only a man anointed with the gift of wisdom; he is Wisdom in person! He is the embodiment and incarnation of divine *sophia*.

The Word of Wisdom

The spiritual gift known as 'the word of wisdom' was not just given to the Lord Jesus, however. Paul teaches in 1 Corinthians 12:8 that the word of wisdom is one of the spiritual gifts which is distributed to members of the Body of Christ by the Holy Spirit. When it is given to a believer, it is given spontaneously and suddenly. It is not something which we discern with the natural mind; it is something unveiled by the power of God's Spirit. The word of wisdom is therefore a charismatic disclosure of divine truth.

With respect to the content of this wisdom, there are essentially two types of insight which the Spirit reveals. The first is theological, and relates to belief. The second is practical, and relates to behaviour. When the first kind of wisdom is administered, it it usually administered in the context of teaching. In other words, a believer is given a special understanding of God's plan of redemption. This is usually given to the believer in difficult circumstances – circumstances involving suffering of one form or another (Luke 21:15). A good example of this kind of 'theological' wisdom can be seen in the following incident involving a conversation between a preacher called Dr Barnhouse and his children:

> Dr Donald Grey Barnhouse told of the occasion when his first wife had died. He was driving his children home from the funeral service. Naturally they were overcome with grief and Dr Barnhouse was trying hard to think of some word of comfort to give them. Just then, a huge truck passed them. As it did so, its shadow swept over the car, and as it passed on in front an idea came to him.
>
> 'Children,' he said, 'would you rather be run over by a truck or by its shadow?' They replied, 'The shadow, of course; that can't hurt us at all'. So Dr Barnhouse then said, 'Did you know that two thousand years ago the truck of death ran over the Lord Jesus ... in order that only its shadow might run over us?'[8]

In this example, the Spirit gave a word of wisdom in a perplexing situation – a word which sheds light on the relationship between God's work of salvation on the cross and a personal tragedy. This is the gift of wisdom in the theological sense, and it is particularly important for teachers (as Origen pointed out in his commentary on Matthew's gospel).

But the word of wisdom can be a practical word as well. The evidence of the first synod of the early Church in Acts 15 supports this. Here the apostle James guides the council into a decision concerning the new Gentile converts which seems good to both the council members and to the Holy Spirit. This is interpreted by Pentecostals as an example of 'the gift of wisdom'. As Cecil Robeck says,

> In Pentecostal circles it [the gift of wisdom] has been commonly understood to be a word of revelation given by the Holy Spirit to provide wisdom to the Christian community at a particular time of need.[9]

An even more obvious example of such practical or pastoral wisdom is Paul's teaching on the gifts of the Spirit itself. Much of 1 Corinthians 14 could be regarded as 'words of wisdom' – as practical guidance for the use (as opposed to the abuse) of the *charismata* in public worship. Here are some examples from 1 Corinthians 14 of Paul's charismatic insights into the use of the grace-gifts:

> Follow the way of love and eagerly desire spiritual gifts (v. 1).

> I would like every one of you to speak in tongues, but I would rather have you prophesy. He who prophesies is greater than one who speaks in tongues, unless he interprets, so that the church may be edified (v. 5).

> For this reason, anyone who speaks in a tongue should pray that he may interpret what he says (v. 13).

> When you come together, everyone has a hymn, a word of instruction, a revelation, a tongue or an interpretation. All of these must be done for the strengthening of the church (v. 26).

> If anyone speaks in a tongue, two – or at the most three – should speak, one at a time, and someone must interpret (v. 27).

If there is no interpreter, the speaker should keep quiet in the church and speak to himself and God (v. 28).

Two or three prophets should speak, and the others should weigh carefully what is said (v. 29).

And if a revelation comes to someone who is sitting down, the first speaker should stop (v. 30).

Everything should be done in a fitting and orderly way (v. 40).

These are fine examples of the practical and ethical form of the word of wisdom. The word of wisdom is, accordingly, a grace-gift which should be eagerly desired by all, and especially by pastors and leaders. In knowing how to deal with difficult situations in church life, pastors and leaders will often need to spend time drawing in the sand, waiting on the Lord, and asking for those 'words of wisdom' which will unveil God's secret purposes.

There are therefore at least two types of wisdom given by the Holy Spirit to a believer. The first is of a theological kind, and relates to what Paul says about God's wisdom in the first two chapters of 1 Corinthians. The second is of a more practical kind, and relates to the kind of wisdom which we see throughout both the Old and the New Testaments – the wisdom for right living. I therefore agree with Rodman Williams' assessment of this gift:

It is apparent that the word of wisdom occupies a high place among the manifestations of the Spirit. For it signifies the speaking forth of a revealing word that centres in Jesus Christ. While it is a mental operation, it is more than a merely rational utterance because it involves deep things that only spiritual eyes and ears can apprehend. Also it adds nothing to Scripture but exposes some depth or height of what Scripture attests. But when such a word is spoken through the Spirit, the Spirit certainly manifests himself and all who hear this word are truly blessed.[10]

The Evaluation of Wisdom

The question remains how we discern wisdom which is truly charismatic from wisdom which is merely human, and how we distinguish between a genuine 'word of wisdom' and something which is, in reality, a word of deception. This was particularly important in the Corinthian situation, where there was a lot of interest in the mystery religions, and where words like 'wisdom' and 'knowledge' were bandied about as the marks of true enlightenment. It is also particularly important in today's world, surrounded as we are with the unmistakable evidence of a growing interest in mystical, esoteric religions and cults. So how do we discern whether a word of wisdom is true or false? Let me suggest a number of issues to address:

1. CONTENT AND CHARACTER

In Corinth, the super-charismatics who gave Paul such a hard time had obviously turned 'wisdom' into a special, spiritual category. Those who had true wisdom were those who thought they understood the mysteries of the universe. They were people who had been initiated into the secrets of the heavenly realms. This suggests to me that the content of their supposedly inspired wisdom was what James Dunn has called an 'insight into the real nature of reality, into the structure of the cosmos and the relationships of divine and human, spiritual and material within that cosmos'. Paul, however, equates 'wisdom' with Jesus Christ. For him, the content of charismatic wisdom is not cosmological but Christological. It stands to reason therefore that a genuine word of wisdom will glorify the Lord Jesus Christ. Furthermore, it will not exalt a truncated Christ – a cosmic Christ with no humanity or historicity. It will exalt Jesus Christ in the totality of his nature and being – pre-existent, incarnate, baptized, crucified, risen, ascended and glorified. As Jonathan Edwards said of manifestations of the Spirit in general:

> When the operation is such as to raise their esteem of that Jesus who was born of the Virgin, and was crucified without the gates of Jerusalem; and seems more to confirm and establish in their minds in the truth of what the Gospel declares to us of his being the Son of

God, and the Saviour of men; it is a sure sign that it is from the Spirit of God.[11]

Paul says in 1 Corinthians 12:3 that it is only by the Holy Spirit that a person can say that Jesus of Nazareth is 'Lord' (i.e. God). If a word of wisdom is Spirit-inspired, it will therefore exalt the Lord Jesus Christ. It will not exalt the person who gives the utterance. It will promote the cause of the Messiah. It will not promote the cause of the messenger.

2. FORM AND FUNCTION

It is very significant to my mind that Paul talks about 'the word' of wisdom. In other words, he stresses that it is something which needs to be spoken out for the benefit of others. By stressing that this gift involves 'utterance', Paul at one stroke undermines the selfishness of those who peddled a different sort of wisdom in the Corinthian church. We can guess that those who regarded themselves as the recipients of spiritual wisdom kept that wisdom to themselves, and regarded it as a special sign of their unique and superior spirituality. The hallmark of inauthentic wisdom was that it was first of all 'kept secret' and secondly used to divide one sort of spiritual person from another. For Paul, however, the exact opposite is true of an authentic word of wisdom. With the genuine article, the first characteristic is that it is verbally communicated rather than jealously guarded. The second is that it is used to edify the community rather than to divide it. Therefore, a genuine word of wisdom will have these two features: it will be shared in love by the one receiving it, and it will have the effect of encouraging and strengthening the Body by giving God's insight and perspective on a complex matter.

3. BELIEF AND BEHAVIOUR

A final point to make is this: that a genuine word of wisdom will be consistent with the truth as it is revealed in Scripture. It will therefore serve to underline, confirm and strengthen our belief in the God of the Bible. It will also encourage behaviour which is wholly consistent with biblical, kingdom ethics. If any purported word of wisdom is not consistent with the Word of God, it must immediately be rejected. As Jonathan Edwards wrote, a genuine work of the Spirit leads us deeper into the truth, not further away from it:

> If by observing the manner of the operation of a spirit that is at work among a people, we see that it operates as a spirit of truth, leading persons to truth, convincing of those things that are true, we may safely determine that it is a right and true spirit ... Whatever spirit removes our darkness, and brings us to the light, undeceives us, and, by convincing us of the truth, doth us a kindness.[12]

This is the hallmark of a true word of wisdom; it provides the Church with an insight into God's general or specific purposes which dispels darkness, deception and confusion, and brings light, comfort and direction in times of need.

Asking for Wisdom

Let us return to where we began. I started this chapter by questioning the popular understanding of the word of wisdom in Charismatic and Pentecostal circles. In common parlance, the word of wisdom is the special ability to apply a word of knowledge in a given situation. While there is probably a relationship between the gifts of wisdom and knowledge (Paul surely sees them as a pair), I do not believe that Paul understood the relationship in these terms. For Paul, the word of wisdom was

> *the articulation of an insight into God's purposes, either general [i.e. to do with God's plan of redemption] or specific [i.e. to do with God's plan for a church or an individual].*

Seen in this light, the grace-gift of wisdom is something far more profound than what we had hitherto supposed. Like 'the word of knowledge', 'the word of wisdom' is primarily a teaching gift. It is the special ability to speak inspirationally of God's purposes at the global, the local or the individual level. In this respect, something of the

teaching gift

'psychic mystique' which surrounds this gift is dispelled. No longer are we talking about a purely intuitive phenomenon but something which involves our minds. Nor are we talking about something to be used by individuals for individuals – a characteristic which surely reflects the rampant individualism in our culture. We are talking about something communal – something which strengthens the belief and the behaviour of the whole community. In short, we are describing something which is to be eagerly desired by the Church.

And how, finally, do we receive this gift? The answer is provided by the apostle James who was, by all accounts, particularly anointed with the gift of wisdom. He wrote,

ask for wisdom and belief

> If any of you lacks wisdom, he should ask God, who gives generously to all without finding fault, and it will be given to him. But when he asks, he must believe and not doubt. (James 1:5–6)

If we need heavenly wisdom, then all we have to do is go to God in prayer, and ask for a word of wisdom in faith. As with all the gifts, trusting in the promises of God is essential. Believing in the extravagant generosity of God is vital. We need to believe in order to receive. So, if you have a real need to understand some aspect of God's purposes, simply pray in faith that the Holy Spirit would give that gift. If you have a desire to see this gift in others, then pray the prayer which Paul prays in Ephesians 1:17:

> I keep asking that the God of our Lord Jesus Christ, the glorious Father, may give you the spirit of wisdom and revelation, so that you may know him better.

Questions

1 Have you ever been given a special insight into the general purposes of God?

2 Has God ever anointed you with a word of wisdom about the cross of Jesus as you witnessed to an unbeliever?

3 Has God ever given you a particularly clear understanding about a subject as you studied and taught his Word?

4   Have you ever heard anyone give a word of wisdom which settled a
    difficult dispute or solved a really complex problem?
5   Are you facing a situation right now in which you require a word of
    wisdom from the Holy Spirit?

Prayer

Lord Jesus Christ, you operated in the gift of wisdom throughout your
ministry. You were truly anointed by the Spirit with wisdom and
understanding, knowledge and discernment. I believe that you are the
source of all godly wisdom, that you indeed are the Wisdom of God.
I ask today that you would give a word of wisdom in the difficult
circumstances which I am now facing. Please confer upon me the spirit
of wisdom and revelation so that I may see your way through my
difficulty. Anoint the leaders of the Church with words of wisdom. I ask
this believing that you have already heard my prayer, and that the
answer is even now on its way. In your name I pray. Amen.

logos → a message, an utterance, inspired speech
        spoken with shimika
sophia → a disclosed secret of Jesus' redemption
         (Gods plan of rescue through the cross)
         in history, and its ethical applications
         in particular moments (between
centers on   legalism and liberalism), especially
Jesus   tragedy

Spend time "drawing in the sand" waiting on
the Lord, praying for wisdom and faith
for it

TWO

The Word of Knowledge

What did Paul mean by 'the word of knowledge'? The answer in popular charismatic contexts is that he meant 'a supernatural insight into the secrets of a person's heart or situation'. Francis Martin says as much when he defines 'the word of knowledge' as follows:

> In our own day, a very special gift, that of knowing what God is doing at this moment in another's soul or body, or knowing of the secrets of another's heart … is often described as a 'word of knowledge'. This gift is particularly common among Pentecostals and those involved in the charismatic movement. The existence of this gift and its divine origin and fruit are unquestionable.[1]

That this 'popular' definition is currently widespread is further confirmed by the descriptions of 'the word of knowledge' in handbooks on the charismatic gifts. Here are two examples from some of the best known authors:

> This is the supernatural revelation of facts about a person or situation, which is not learned through the efforts of the natural mind, but is a fragment of knowledge freely given by God, disclosing the truth which the Spirit wishes to be made known concerning a particular person or situation. (David Pytches)[2]

I believe that the word of knowledge is a thought, or impression on our mind, or a vision or the direct audible voice of the Holy Spirit ABOUT a situation. (Bill Subritsky)[3]

The story which is often used as an example of this particular gift is one involving John Wimber:

I was once on an airplane when I turned and looked at a passenger across the aisle to see the word 'adultery' written across his face in big letters. The letters, of course, were only perceptible to spiritual eyes. He caught me looking at him (gaping might be more descriptive) and said 'What do you want?' As he asked that, a woman's name came clearly into my mind. I leaned over the aisle and asked if the name meant anything to him. His face turned pale and he asked if he could talk to me.

It was a large plane with a bar, so we went there to talk. On the way the Lord spoke to me again, saying 'Tell him to turn from his adulterous affair or I'm going to take him.'

When we got to the bar I told him that God had told me that he was committing adultery with the woman whose name God had revealed to me and that God would take him if he did not repent. He melted on the spot, and asked what he should do. I led him through a prayer of repentance and he received Christ. This was in front of a stewardess and two other passengers, who were shocked, but then also began to cry.

Then he said that his wife was downstairs in the seat next to his. I told him to go and tell her the entire story, which he did. He led her to Christ.[4]

In this chapter I would like to offer a different understanding of 'the word of knowledge'. My conviction is that the popular understanding of this gift is mistaken. To be sure, the word of knowledge is, like all the grace-gifts in 1 Corinthians 12:8–10, a *spiritual* anointing. In this respect I agree with Rod Williams' assessment of the *charismata* in general:

Gifts of the Holy Spirit are not latent natural talents or trained abilities brought to heightened expression. The spiritual gifts are by no means more of what is already present, no matter how elevated. They are not simply an added spiritual injection that causes talents and abilities to function with greater effectiveness … they are gifts of the Spirit, endowments, not enhancements.[5]

The knowledge referred to in the gift of knowledge is, accordingly, not a 'general knowledge' acquired through learning, or even biblical knowledge gained through research. It is a revealed knowledge imparted by the grace of God and *kata to auto pneuma* ('by means of the same Spirit', 1 Corinthians 12:8). In that sense it is a spiritual insight. At the same time, the popular understanding of this gift as an insight *into a person's thoughts* needs correcting. As we will see in a moment, other passages in 1 Corinthians would suggest that 'the word of knowledge' is an insight into God's thoughts, not ours! With that in mind, I would like to propose an alternative definition of 'the word of knowledge':

> *the word of knowledge is an inspired insight into the mind of Christ which is then expressed in words given by the Holy Spirit. As such, it is a revelatory gift through which the Body of Christ is edified.*

A Question of Method

A word is needed at this point about method. It would not be unfair to say that the methodology employed in the context of this particular gift has often been faulty. Two problems spring to mind in this regard. First, there has been a tendency to interpret this grace-gift in the light of personal experience alone. Pentecostals and Charismatics commonly receive divine revelation about other people. I myself have had this experience. The problem is that we tend to go to the Scriptures in order to look for a similar phenomenon, and then force that text into the mould of our own experience. However, this is the exact opposite of what we should be doing. We should be going to biblical passages which describe charismatic revelation, interpreting those passages responsibly and accurately, and then defining our experience in the light of what the Word teaches us. We must therefore be careful about our methodology. It is a well-known saying in Pentecostal circles that the man with a theology is at the mercy of a man with an experience. That is, in practice, often true. However, we must take great care not to allow our personal experience to take precedence over what the Bible teaches. In reality, the two need to inform each other in a rigorous and critical way, with the Word of God taking priority in terms of authority.

A second methodological error concerns the basic rules of biblical interpretation. So often people who teach about the word of knowledge interpret what Paul meant with reference to books in the Bible not written by Paul! Thus, the classic example of knowledge which is often quoted is the incident involving Jesus and the Samaritan woman in John 4:4–42. There Jesus receives a revelation concerning the woman's secret history of sin, and tells her that she has had five husbands and is living with a sixth man. This, it is claimed, is what Paul meant by 'the word of knowledge'. The problem here is that we are interpreting what Paul meant with reference to John's gospel! Instead of asking how Paul uses the word 'knowledge' in 1 Corinthians, we look elsewhere in the New Testament to find passages which legitimate our own experience of what we feel this gift ought to be. But this is not responsible interpretation. The right way is to start with what Paul says about the gift in 1 Corinthians 12:8 and then to infer what he might have meant with reference to the rest of the letter.

Knowledge in 1 Corinthians

Let us therefore begin by studying other references to 'knowledge' in 1 Corinthians. Straightaway we discover that there is one other passage in the letter where Paul talks about a kind of knowledge which is revealed by the Holy Spirit and then articulated in words. In chapter 2, Paul describes the revelation which comes from the Spirit. He says that God has revealed his mind to believers, and that he has done that by his Spirit. Unbelievers cannot receive this revelation because they are fundamentally 'unspiritual'. They have not received the Holy Spirit. Believers, on the other hand, are spiritual people. They are people whose minds are so saturated with the Spirit of God that they can understand spiritual truths and indeed express such truths in words given by the Holy Spirit. They are people who know the mind of the Lord Jesus Christ. Here is the relevant passage:

> The Spirit searches all things, even the deep things of God. For who among men knows the thoughts of a man except the man's spirit within him? In the same way no one knows the thoughts of God except the Spirit of God. We have not received the spirit of the world but the Spirit who is from God, *that we may understand what God has freely given us. This is what we speak, not in words taught us by human wisdom, but in words taught by the Spirit, expressing spiritual truths in spiritual words.* (Italics mine.)

It is within this passage that Paul speaks about something which sounds like 'the word of knowledge'. In verses 12–13 he writes about a knowledge of things which God has freely given us. That knowledge is given by the Holy Spirit, and it is then articulated in words given by the Spirit. In this statement there are a number of parallels with 1 Corinthians 12:8, where Paul speaks about *logos gnoseos kata to auto pneuma* – a word of knowledge given by the same Spirit. The word *logos* should be translated as 'utterance'. It denotes something which is 'put into words'. The word *gnoseos* is the genitive singular of *gnosis*, which should be translated 'knowledge'. The words *kata to auto pneuma* should be translated 'by means of the same Spirit'. In 1 Corinthians 12:8 three things are indicated about the gift of knowledge: its expression ('an utterance'), its content ('knowledge') and its agency ('Spirit').

In 1 Corinthians 2:12–13, Paul speaks of a similar phenomenon. He first of all says that believers have received 'the Spirit that is from God', and that one of the functions of the Spirit is to help us to *know* the things that God has freely given. The Greek verb translated 'know' or 'understand' is *eidon*, which is a synonym for *ginoskein* – the verb form of the word *gnosis*, used of the word of 'knowledge'. Both verbs mean 'to know'. Thus Paul is speaking here of knowledge imparted by the Holy Spirit.

Secondly, Paul talks about the content of this knowledge in 'charismatic' language. He says that this inspired knowledge concerns 'the things that God has freely given us'. The verb translated 'freely given' is a translation of *ta charisthenta*, which comes from the same root as *charisma*, meaning 'grace-gift'. Thus, the content of this inspired knowledge is the gracious work of Almighty God. It is a revelation of the thoughts of God, not the thoughts of a man (1 Corinthians 2:11).

Thirdly, Paul says that this inspired knowledge of God's secret thoughts is put into words which are taught to us by the Spirit. The word translated 'words' is *logois*, the same noun used in 1 Corinthians 12:8 for the 'word' of knowledge. Thus, in 1 Corinthians 2:12–13, Paul talks about a knowledge of God's grace which is revealed by the Holy Spirit and then expressed in 'words taught by the Spirit'. In defining the grace-gift known as 'the word of knowledge', it seems to me that we need look no further than 1 Corinthians 2:12–13 for help. This passage suggests that the word of knowledge is a *special anointing in which a believer is given an insight into the unfathomable depths of God's grace – an insight which he or she then articulates in words taught by the Holy Spirit.*

Knowledge of what God has freely given us

The Content of Knowledge

What did Paul mean when he wrote that the Spirit enables us to know 'the things that God has freely given us'? Answering this question is vital because it will enable us to understand more precisely what kind of knowledge Paul is talking about when he speaks of this particular gift.

As with the 'word of wisdom', I propose that Paul has in mind two kinds of knowledge, the first *theological* and the second *practical.* When Paul talks about knowledge of the things that God has freely 'given' us (*charisthena*), we are reminded of the word *charisma.* In the introduction to this book I showed how Paul uses the noun *charisma* in two ways. The first refers to the supreme example of God's grace – the free gift of eternal life through our Lord Jesus Christ (see, for example, Romans 6:23). When Paul speaks of 'the word of knowledge', I therefore propose that he first of all means the articulation of an inspired insight into the ultimate demonstration of the grace of God, the gift of his Son to the world. The word of knowledge understood in the theological sense is therefore *the anointed description of one of the many treasures associated with God's gracious gift of his Son.*

What, then, of the secondary, practical sense of this word? Here we need to keep in mind that Paul uses the word *charisma* in a specific as well as a general sense. The word *charisma* is Paul's favourite term for the grace-gifts of the Holy Spirit, described in 1 Corinthians 12:8. When Paul says in 2:12–13 that the Spirit enables us to know and to describe the things that God has freely given us, it is quite probable that he is not only thinking of the supreme *charisma* of God's Son, but also of the more specific *charismata*, the manifestations of the Spirit mentioned later on: the word of wisdom, word of knowledge, faith, gifts of healing, miracles, prophecy, discernment, tongues, interpretation. The word of knowledge understood in the pastoral sense would then be *an anointed description of the work of grace available to the Church of Jesus Christ.* In this respect I agree with James Dunn:

> 'Word of knowledge' ... would denote some charismatic insight into 'the things given us by God' ... that is, some understanding of the relationship of God to the believer(s), some recognition of the charismatic dimension ... to the believer's life individually and as a community.[6]

Knowledge and Teaching

This definition of the word of knowledge departs from the norm; instead of seeing it as a revelation of a person's secrets, we now see it as an inspired utterance concerning God's works of grace. These works of grace apply generally to the supreme *charisma*, the gracious gift of God's Son. In this respect, 'the word of knowledge' is an invaluable tool for those who are called to teach in the Church. It is the special ability to speak in an inspirational way of the wide range of blessings which God has given us through Jesus Christ. As John Rea has put it:

> In this sense a word of knowledge may be manifested when the teacher receives a new insight into the knowledge of God or of the Christian faith and at the same time is given new ability to express it and explain it to others.[7]

Do we have any examples of such 'words of knowledge' in the New Testament? Once we understand the word of knowledge as 'the special ability to speak inspirationally of the general *charisma* of God', then the answer is 'yes'. Perhaps the finest example is Paul's prayer in Ephesians 1:3–14. In the Greek, this prayer proceeds for 26 lines before we reach a full stop. It is a breathless, enthusiastic and fervent expression of gratitude for 'the things which God has freely given to us'. Indeed, in the middle of the prayer, Paul speaks of the 'grace' (*charis*) with which God has 'graced' us (*echaritosen*). The verb translated 'graced' or favoured' is only used twice in the New Testament – here, of believers in general, and in Luke 1:28, of Mary the mother of Jesus. We are accustomed to thinking of Mary as 'highly favoured'. We are not so used to thinking of ourselves in the same light. Yet Paul insists in his prayer that all believers are favoured with the grace of God. Indeed, in vv. 7–8 Paul can hardly contain himself as he speaks of 'the riches of God's grace which he *lavished* on us'.

Paul's prayer in Ephesians 1:3–14 is a wonderful example of 'the word of knowledge'. Indeed, the whole passage consists of one 'word of knowledge' after another – one charismatic insight into God's grace after another. Paul begins by blessing God for the many blessings that are given to the believer:

> Blessed be the God and Father of our Lord Jesus Christ,
> who has blessed us in the heavenly realms with every
> spiritual blessing in Christ (v. 3).

Here Paul begins by praising the Trinitarian God – the Father, the Lord Jesus Christ, and the Spirit who gives blessings. The rest of the prayer identifies the gracious gifts given by each member of the Trinity. The first part of the prayer identifies those gifts which are given by the Father (vv. 4–6):

> He chose us
> He predestined us to be adopted
> He freely gave us his glorious grace.

In the second part of the prayer, Paul gives thanks for the gifts given by the Son (vv. 7–13):

> In him we have redemption, the forgiveness of sins
> In him we were chosen
> and included.

In the third part of the prayer, Paul gives thanks for the gifts given by the Spirit (vv. 13–14):

> You were marked with a seal,
> The promised Holy Spirit
> The deposit guaranteeing our inheritance.

Here, then, we see a beautiful example of words of knowledge in the theological sense. Clearly Paul was given a profound revelation of 'the things which God has freely given us' (1 Corinthians 2:12), and articulates this charismatic knowledge in 'words taught by the Spirit'. Truly, the one called to teach cannot afford to neglect so great a gift as this. Teachers need 'the word of knowledge' if they are to know 'the mystery of God's good pleasure' (Ephesians 1:9), the hope to which he has called us, the riches of his glorious inheritance, his incomparably great power (Ephesians 1:18–19) and the love that surpasses knowledge (Ephesians 3:19). Such knowledge only comes through the power of the Holy Spirit.

Knowledge and Pastoring

The word of knowledge is therefore that special ability to know and to articulate the things which God has freely given to us. In the first instance, this refers to the spiritual anointing by which a teacher, or, indeed, any member of the Body of Christ, is enabled to know the *charisma* of God in the general sense. What then of the practical application of this gift? Here we proceed to the specific sense of the word *charisma*, which refers to the 'grace-gifts' given for the upbuilding of the Body of Christ. The New Testament makes it clear that God intends us to have knowledge of his *charisma* in this specific sense. That is why Paul states that he does not want anyone to be uninformed about the gifts of the Spirit (1 Corinthians 12:1). It follows, therefore, that there is a practical as well as a theological application to the word of knowledge. The practical aspect can be defined as *the inspired ability to understand the nature and the function of the gifts of the Holy Spirit.*

This thought brings us back to 1 Corinthians 12, and to Paul's teaching on the spiritual gifts. Have you ever paused to consider where the information in this chapter, and indeed in chapters 13 and 14, came from? Are these Paul's own ideas, based on his own rational speculation about the spiritual gifts? Or are they examples of inspired speech? From a charismatic perspective, the answer must be that much of what Paul says about the *charismata* in these chapters is itself charismatic. In other words, while discussing gifts such as 'the word of wisdom' and 'the word of knowledge', Paul is himself operating in these gifts as he writes to the Corinthian church. In the last chapter we saw that with particular reference to the word of wisdom. A great deal of the counsel given by Paul about the use of the gifts constitutes 'wisdom' in the practical, charismatic sense. Whenever Paul describes how to use these gifts responsibly, he is demonstrating that he himself is anointed with wisdom. Whenever Paul describes what these gifts actually are, he is demonstrating that he himself is anointed with knowledge. So when Paul deals with the 'what' he is operating in the gift of knowledge. When he is describing the 'how', he is operating in the gift of wisdom.

In 1 Corinthians 12–14, there are numerous examples of 'words of knowledge' in the pastoral sense. These refer to 'the things given freely by God' in the more specific sense of the grace-gifts. Here are a few examples of the kind of charismatic insight into the grace-gifts which Paul receives from the Holy Spirit and then passes on to the church:

No one can say 'Jesus is Lord' except by the Holy
Spirit. (12:1)

There are different kinds of gifts, but the same Spirit.
There are different kinds of service, but the same Lord.
There are different kinds of working, but the same God
works all of them in all men. (12:4–6)

Now to each one the manifestation of the Spirit is given
for the common good. (12:7)

All these are the work of one and the same Spirit, and he
gives them to each one, just as he determines. (12:11)

If I have the gift of prophecy and can fathom all mysteries
and all knowledge, and if I have a faith that can move
mountains, but have not love, I am nothing. (13:2)

Where there are prophecies, they will cease; where there are
tongues, they will be stilled; where there is knowledge,
it will pass away. (13:8)

He who speaks in a tongue edifies himself, but he who
prophecies edifies the church. (14:3)

When we ask where Paul acquired this understanding of the grace-gifts, we are forced to recognize that this is not human knowledge. Rather, it is inspired knowledge. These words in which the gifts of grace are described for us are, indeed, 'words of knowledge'. Thus the *form* of Paul's writing is as charismatic as the *content* in these chapters.

Wisdom and Knowledge

At this point it is important to explore the connection between the two gifts of wisdom and knowledge. At least some of the spiritual gifts in Paul's list in 1 Corinthians 12 seem to be paired together. Of these, the most obvious 'couplings' of gifts are:

wisdom and knowledge
prophecy and discernment
tongues and interpretation

The relationship between prophecy and discernment is obvious. We need discernment if we are to evaluate whether a prophecy is authentic or not. The relationship between tongues and interpretation is equally obvious. We need a public message in tongues to be translated into our native language if it is to be comprehensible. What, then, of wisdom and knowledge? Is there a similar relationship between these two?

In terms of wisdom and knowledge in the theological sense, the differences between the two are not clear. Wisdom seems to be connected with the ability to understand God's secret purposes, which Paul describes as a 'mystery'. Knowledge seems to be related to 'the things which God has freely given us', which Paul relates to 'grace'. If Paul knows of a stark distinction between these two kinds of revelation he is not explicit about it. However, when the grace-gifts themselves are the object, wisdom seems to refer to the way in which we are to use the gifts, while knowledge seems to refer to the nature of the gifts. If that is a correct interpretation, then wisdom is associated with 'how' and knowledge with 'what'. In the light of this, it may therefore be right to infer that theological knowledge refers to insights into God's grace, while theological wisdom refers to insights concerning the way that grace is worked out, particularly in the Cross.

Whatever the differences between the two gifts, the similarities need to be stressed as well. Both gifts are gifts of utterance. Paul prefaces both with the word *logos*, meaning 'speech'. Thus, both gifts are examples of inspired speech. Both gifts are also 'pneumatic' in character. That is to say, they are manifestations of the Holy

Spirit, not of human wisdom or knowledge. Paul emphasizes this truth by saying that the word of wisdom is given *dia tou pneumatos* (through the Spirit), while the word of knowledge is given *kata to auto pneuma* (by means of the same Spirit). Both gifts are therefore the result of divine illumination, even though the human mind is not bypassed by either. Finally, both gifts are temporary; they will disappear at the *parousia*:

> Where there is knowledge, it will pass away. For we know in part, and we prophesy in part, but when the end comes, the imperfect disappears ... Now I know in part; then I shall know fully, even as I am fully known.
>
> (1 Corinthians 13:8–12)

Knowledge and Prophecy

What then, of the popular definition of 'the word of knowledge' in Pentecostal and Charismatic teaching? Can a 'word of knowledge' ever be interpreted as a charismatic insight into the hidden facts about a person's life? Is there any basis in Scripture for such a view of this gift? My own view is that the phenomenon described by many Pentecostals as 'the gift of knowledge' is, in reality, an aspect of the gift of prophecy. The common view that the gift of knowledge is a revelation of a person's secrets should therefore be revised. This is confirmed even within the teaching of 1 Corinthians 12–14. When Paul is describing the effects of public prophecy on unbelievers who are present in the assembly, he writes the following:

> If an unbeliever or someone who does not understand comes in while everybody is prophesying, he will be convinced by all that he is a sinner and will be judged by all, and the secrets of his heart will be laid bare. So he will fall down and worship God, exclaiming, 'God is really among you!'
>
> (1 Corinthians 14:24–25)

Prophecy

This is prophecy — what some typically call a manifestation of knowledge

The spiritual gift which is being described in this passage is prophecy, and it is this rather than 'the word of knowledge' which is said
to uncover the secrets of an unbeliever's heart. Thus, the phenomenon of *kardiagnosis*, of revealed knowledge of the heart, is more
properly speaking a characteristic of prophecy than of the word of
knowledge.[8] Even the example in John's gospel – so often quoted in
this regard – bears this out. When Jesus tells the Samaritan woman
that she has had five husbands and is living with a sixth man, she
does not reply by saying, 'Sir, I see you have the gift of knowledge!'
She replies, 'Sir, I can see that you are a *prophet*' (John 4:19). Now
there may be an element of overlap between knowledge and
prophecy, as there is in the case of a number of the gifts. But it does
seem more accurate to identify such pneumatic knowledge with
prophecy rather than any of the other gifts. With this in mind, I
agree with the view expressed by Wayne Grudem:

> What many people today call 'word of wisdom' and 'word of knowl-
> edge' in charismatic circles, it would seem better simply to refer to as
> 'prophecy'.[9]

The Praxis of the Gift

Where, then, does this lead us? It leads to a revised understanding
of 'the word of knowledge' in Pentecostal and Charismatic praxis.
In this chapter I have sought to begin with a theological-exegetical
description of the gift of knowledge rather than a description of
experiences of divine revelation. This has led us to the conclusion
that Paul's understanding of 'the word of knowledge' is to be
defined as *the special ability to put into words divinely revealed knowledge about God's grace*. In arriving at this definition, we have found
Paul's words in 1 Corinthians 2:12–13 to be a key clue for the
correct interpretation of this particular 'manifestation of the Spirit'.
There Paul speaks of Spirit-filled people being given inspired knowledge of 'the things which God has freely given us', and an equally
inspired ability to teach such spiritual truths in words taught by the
Spirit. Using this background I have proposed that the content of

'the word of knowledge' is the grace of God. At the general theological level, this means the kind of *charisma* described in Romans 6:23 – 'the free gift (*charisma*) of God is eternal life through our Lord Jesus Christ.' At the specific, pastoral level, this means the kind of *charisma* described in 1 Corinthians 12–14 – the grace-gifts of the Holy Spirit. Thus,

> *the word of knowledge is a special anointing in which a believer is given revelation concerning the gracious works of God which he then articulates in words taught by the Holy Spirit.*

If we now look at the actual experience of Pentecostals and Charismatics, we can see that this kind of definition makes sense of a good deal of what is manifested in both groups. If we take the 'word of knowledge' in the general, theological sense first, it is immediately noticeable in the early days of Asuza Street[10] how relatively uneducated men and women were enabled by God to speak with extraordinary insight about the operations of divine grace. Reading Frank Bartleman's account of *What Really Happened at Asuza Street?* is an instructive exercise in this respect. On just about every page there are insights into the gracious ways in which God works amongst his people – insights that could only have been revealed by the Holy Spirit. Bartleman himself indicates as much when he contrasts the intellectual knowledge of God with revealed knowledge:

> The greater part of most Christian's knowledge of God is and always has been, since the loss of the Spirit by the early Church, an intellectual knowledge. Their knowledge of the Word and principles of God is an intellectual one, through natural reasoning and understanding largely. They have little revelation, illumination or inspiration direct from the Spirit of God.[11]

Bartleman's view was that the human mind is the last fortress of man to yield. He wrote that our self-assertiveness, natural wisdom and self-sufficiency have to be crucified before the Holy Spirit can impart revealed knowledge to us.

People like Bartleman therefore resolved to have their minds sanctified and then fully yielded to the Holy Spirit. They spent much time on their own in prayer, studying Scripture and church history, and listening out for the revelation of the Holy Spirit in what they called 'the holy of holies' – the place of quiet waiting upon the Lord. It was in that attitude of mind, and within the context of this kind of spiritual discipline, that such men and women received 'the word of knowledge'. They were given a special ability to know the things which God freely gives to us by his grace. For this reason they could utter insights which are unattainable by the 'unspiritual' man. Witness, for example, the 'knowledge' in the following extract from Bartleman's book:

> God is not trying to build up something else, or to do something for men that will make them great and mighty, but rather to bring all men to naught, and do the work through the power of the Holy Ghost. The call of God to his people now is to humble themselves; to recognize their weakness and lack of power, to get down before him, and wait till his power is restored. The great question is, will men see the plan of God, and yield to it? Will men get down in humility at Jesus' feet, and pray and wait till he restores his full, Pentecostal power? Or will they continue to run ahead of him, and fail in the end?[12]

Here we see precisely the kind of 'word of knowledge' which I have been describing in this chapter. It is a word clearly born out of times of prayerful listening. Indeed, Bartleman himself wrote that

> Only the man who lives in fellowship with divine reality can be used to call the people to God.[13]

In these times of prayer, the Holy Spirit revealed 'words of knowledge' concerning the things which God freely gives to his people in times of revival. More specifically, insights were also given about the nature and the operation of the grace-gifts of the Spirit. Thus Bartleman could write the following 'words of knowledge':

Don't allow the devil to rob you of a real 'Pentecost'. Any work that exalts the Holy Ghost or the 'gifts' above Jesus will finally end up in fanaticism. Whatever causes us to exalt and love Jesus is well and safe. The reverse will ruin all. The Holy Ghost is a great light, but focused on Jesus always, for his revealing ... Everything centres around Jesus. We may not put the power, gifts, the Holy Ghost, or in fact anything ahead of Jesus. Any mission that exalts the Holy Ghost above the Lord Jesus Christ is bound for the rocks of error...[14]

It is this kind of charismatic insight into the workings of God's grace which I believe Paul meant by the word of knowledge. Such insights, wherever they are given, succeed in giving much needed revelation and guidance to the Church. Of course every claim to revelation should be tested, particularly in the light of Scripture. If they are not consistent with Scripture, if they do not build up the Church, and if they do not glorify Jesus, then they are to be rejected out of hand. But when such insights are truly given by the Holy Spirit, and expressed in spiritual and loving words, then their fruit is worthwhile indeed. So may God help us to become more and more open to receiving and using this gift of 'the word of knowledge', to the glory of Jesus Christ, and for the enrichment of his Church.

Questions

1 How have you interpreted the word of knowledge in the past?
2 Do you think the interpretation of this gift should be based on our experience or on what Scripture reveals?
3 How has your perspective changed as a result of reading this chapter?
4 Do you feel that you need more insight into the things that God freely gives us?
5 How responsible and biblical is your church in the handling of the grace-gifts of the Spirit?
6 Is your knowledge of God more intellectual than spiritual?
7 Can you think of examples of 'the word of knowledge' in your own experience?

Prayer

Lord Jesus Christ, I thank you for 'the word of knowledge'. I pray that you would make me more and more receptive to receiving insights into your gracious works. Make me more aware of what your Spirit is saying. Give me eyes to see, ears to hear, and a mind to understand. Where the Church needs 'words of knowledge', please would you provide them. Help us always to remember that the treasures of wisdom and knowledge are hidden in you. In your name. Amen.

logos → utterance

gnoseos → knowledge of what God has freely given us, the treasures associated with the gift of God's Son, an anointed description of a work of grace available to the church (the substance of Ephesian prayer)

Depend on God for this → Pray the Ephesians prayer!

THREE

The Gift of Faith

In the year 538 BC, God raised up a man by the name of Zerubbabel. His task was to lead 50,000 Jews from their exile in Babylon back to the land of Judah. Zerubbabel achieved this task, and on arriving at the site of the sacked city of Jerusalem, started the reconstruction of the Temple. For two years the people worked hard. They completed the bronze altar of sacrifice, and started to make sacrifices once again (Ezra 3:1–6). They then rebuilt the foundations of the Temple (Ezra 3:7–13). However, in 536 BC, the work ground to a halt. There were two reasons for this. There was first of all the problem of external antagonism. The people who lived around Jerusalem set about discouraging those involved in the building project, with the result that the builders became afraid (Ezra 4:4). Secondly, there was the problem of internal anxiety. A number of the older priests, Levites and family heads could remember the former Temple, and they started to moan that Zerubbabel's Temple would not be as glorious (Ezra 3:12). The combined effects of external antagonism and internal anxiety succeeded in postponing the work.

For sixteen years there was no further building. The 50,000 who had come back from exile turned from building a beautiful house for God to building beautiful houses for themselves (Haggai 1:3–4). However, in 520 BC, God anointed the prophet Zechariah to go to Zerubbabel with a word of encouragement. The gist of Zechariah's message is this (Zechariah 4):

You, Zerubbabel, and your fellow leader Joshua, are two men appointed by the Lord to serve his purposes. God promises that you will complete the work which you have begun on the Temple. Indeed, your hands have laid the foundations, and your hands will finish the work. As you bring out the capstone, the last stone to be put into place, all the people will cry out, 'Isn't it lovely? Isn't it lovely?' So, in the meantime, be encouraged. The obstacles before you may feel like a mountain of impossibilities, but God is going to level that mountain. As you rely on the power of the Spirit rather than on your own resources, God will do the work and you will see the Temple rebuilt. Today may be a day of small things, but you are not to despise that.

Evidently Zerubbabel responded to this word of encouragement, and indeed to a similar word recorded in the two chapters of the Book of Haggai. In 520 BC, the rebuilding started once again. The Temple and its courts were built, and by 516 BC the Temple of Zerubbabel was completed. The mountain of opposition had indeed been moved, levelled by the Spirit of the Lord. The key to the breakthrough in all this was Zerubbabel himself. Before the Temple could be restored, Zerubbabel had to be restored, and this personal restoration was mostly to do with faith. Zerubbabel needed to exchange faith in his own abilities for a mountain-moving faith in the resources of God. In short, he had to learn to trust in the Holy Spirit rather than in himself. As the prophet Zechariah told him,

'Not by human might, nor by human strength, but by my Spirit (*ruach*)' says the Lord Almighty.

The Gift of Faith

In the list of the grace-gifts in 1 Corinthians 12:8–10, Paul writes about the kind of faith which was given to Zerubbabel. He says that 'to another is given faith by the same Spirit'. Faith is therefore one of the manifestations of the Spirit. In defining what this gift of faith is, we need to look at what Paul says about faith elsewhere in 1 Corinthians 12–14. In the context of these chapters there is only one other reference to what might be called the 'gift of faith'. That is in chapter 13, where Paul says the following:

> If I have the gift of prophecy and can fathom all mysteries and knowledge, and if I have a faith that can move mountains, but have not love, I am nothing (v. 2).

Is the allusion to 'mountain-moving faith' a reference to 'the gift of faith'? Two factors indicate that it is. First of all, the word Paul uses for faith (*pistis*) is exactly the same word which he uses when he speaks of the gift of faith. Secondly, and more convincing, is the fact that the other phenomena mentioned in the above quotation are gifts of the Spirit. Paul speaks of the gift of prophecy, the ability to fathom all mysteries (i.e. 'the word of wisdom') and knowledge (i.e. 'the word of knowledge'). It stands to reason that if these three are gifts of the Spirit, then 'mountain-moving faith' is as well.

The gift of faith is, accordingly, an unshakeable confidence that God can move any obstacle, however great or small. It is the kind of confidence in the *ruach ha-kodesh* (the Holy Spirit) which God gave to Zerubbabel. It is the same kind of faith which Jesus teaches about in Mark 11:22–25, when the apostles enquire how Jesus caused the fig-tree to wither:

> 'Have faith in God,' Jesus answered. 'I tell you the truth, if anyone says to this mountain, "Go, throw yourself into the sea," and does not doubt in his heart but believes that what he says will happen, it will be done for him. Therefore I tell you, whatever you ask for in prayer, believe that you have received it, and it will be yours. And when you stand praying, if you hold anything against anyone, forgive him, so that your Father in heaven may forgive you your sins.'

In this passage, Jesus speaks about the faith that can move a mountain. We will look in more detail at this teaching later, but for now the important thing to notice is that this is precisely the kind of quality which Paul describes in 1 Corinthians 12:9 and 13:2. Paul talks about the 'gift of faith', which he later defines as 'a faith that can move mountains'. He is therefore speaking of the same power-ful phenomenon as Jesus.

In defining this grace-gift of faith, we need to understand it in the context of the rest of the spiritual gifts. In that respect, three things need to be emphasized. First of all, this gift, like the other gifts, is not given to every member of the Body of Christ, but is given to some, as the Spirit determines. Paul states that 'to another' is given the gift of faith. He does not say 'to everyone'. So the first point to remember concerns the extent of this gift. The distribution of this charismatic endowment is not universal. It is selective, and the process of 'supernatural selection' is dependent upon the sovereign-ty of God, not upon our own plans and desires.

Secondly, we need to remember the origin of the gift of faith. This faith, like all the gifts, is a manifestation of the Spirit. It is not the result of human motivation but of pneumatic empowerment. Paul stresses this by saying that 'to another [is given] faith *by the same Spirit*' (*en to auto pneumati*). Just as the gift of wisdom is given 'through the Spirit' (*dia tou pneumatos*), and just as the gift of knowledge is given 'by means of the same Spirit' (*kata to auto pneuma*), so faith is given 'by' the Spirit. The gift of faith is therefore not 'positive thinking', to use a current phrase in New Age psychology. It is an example of the energy of God's Spirit at work in our lives (1 Corinthians 12:6). With that in mind, I agree totally with Professor James Dunn's definition of this gift:

> Paul presumably has in mind that mysterious surge of confidence which sometimes arises within a man in a particular situation of need or challenge and which gives him an otherly certainty that God is about to act through a word or through an action (such as laying hands on someone sick).[1]

Thirdly, we need to take note of the 'purpose' of the gift of faith. Dunn's definition links this gift with healing. That is surely correct. Paul's list of the *charismata* in 1 Corinthians 12:8–10 can be divided in the following way:

1 Gifts of Teaching – wisdom and knowledge
2 Gifts of Power – faith, healing, miracles
3 Gifts of Revelation – prophecy and discernment
4 Gifts of Adoration – tongues and interpretation

The fact that Paul follows 'faith' with the gifts of healing and miraculous works indicates that he himself sees a connection between the three. Indeed, Paul probably saw the gift of faith as a powerful anointing for those involved in the healing ministry and those he calls 'workers of miracles' (1 Corinthians 12:28). It may be that he saw this gift as a sudden surge of confidence that God would move the mountains of sickness, oppression, poverty, opposition and so on. If that is so, then the 'purpose' of this gift, like all the gifts, is to strengthen the Body of Christ, particularly in the context of healing and miraculous works.

To sum up: *the gift of faith is a supernatural certainty given by the Holy Spirit to some members of the Body of Christ. This certainty is an unshakeable confidence that God is about to resolve a seemingly impossible situation, for the edification of the Church.*

Conversion Faith

With this in mind it is important that we distinguish 'charismatic faith' from two other kinds of faith which are referred to throughout the New Testament. The first of these is what I call 'conversion' faith. Conversion faith is basically the faith that justifies us before God. It is the faith in God's grace which leads to our salvation. Paul says in Ephesians 2:8–9 that it is

By grace you have been saved, through faith – and this not from yourselves, it is the gift of God – not by works, so that no one can boast.

Salvation from sin therefore occurs when a person believes that the grace of God has accomplished what human effort could not – namely, divine forgiveness and pardon. The grace of God is essentially God's unmerited favour and compassion. This divine grace is most perfectly demonstrated in the death of God's one and only Son on the cross – a death which provides the perfect atonement for sin. The teaching of the New Testament is clear on this: we are saved from our sins when we truly believe that God has, through the gracious sacrifice of his Son, done what we could not do through good works and religious duties; he has provided the means by which we can – in the words of the hymn – be 'ransomed, healed, restored, forgiven'. Conversion faith is therefore faith in the *pardon* of Jesus. It is a matter of believing that Jesus has done everything necessary for our salvation on the cross.

Secondly, conversion faith is faith in the *person* of Jesus. At this point it is necessary to move outside the writings of Paul, and to consider the New Testament as a whole. In John's gospel, the verb 'to believe' (*pisteuein*) is used 98 times. John uses this verb to reveal that there is a content to our faith. For example, he uses the verb with the word *hoti*, meaning 'that ...' A good example of *pisteuein* with the word *hoti* is in John 20:31:

> These things have been written in order that you may believe (*pisteuein*) that (*hoti*) Jesus is the Christ ...

Here the need to believe in the *person* of Jesus is indicated. Conversion faith requires that we believe that Jesus of Nazareth was and is *Christos* – i.e. the Messiah – and indeed God's Son (John 11:27). More than that, it means believing that Jesus came from God (John 16:27), that God sent Jesus to the world (John 11:42; 17:8), and that Jesus is the 'I AM' of God (John 8:24; 13:19). Thus, conversion faith is faith in the *person* of Jesus. It involves believing certain things about Jesus, for example, his divine origin, name and nature. It also involves complete trust in Jesus Christ (hence John's use of the construction *pisteuein eis* ... to believe in). As Leon Morris puts it, 'believing in Jesus is the critical thing'.

So then, conversion faith is the faith that saves and justifies. It involves a wholehearted faith in the *person* of Jesus and an equally committed trust in the *pardon* of Jesus.

For myself, I know that the moment of my conversion occurred when I was seventeen years old. After a long struggle with God, I eventually surrendered. I recognized that I was a sinner, and that I needed a brand new start. In short, I recognized my need to be born again. At the same time, God had been giving me increasing faith in Jesus. I grew more and more to believe that Jesus was the Son of God, that he died on the cross for my sins, and that he was beckoning me to follow him for the rest of my days. I therefore went round to the home of a Christian teacher and told him of the decision that I wanted to make. After an initial reaction of surprise, the teacher invited me into his house and explained the Gospel in simple terms. He asked me whether I believed that Jesus was the Son of God, and I said 'yes'. He asked whether I believed that Jesus died for my sins, and I said 'yes'. He asked whether I believed that Jesus had been raised from death and is alive today, and again I said 'yes'. Finally, he asked whether I believed that Jesus is Lord of all, including my own life, and I answered, 'yes'. We then prayed together, and I went home that night feeling as though real life — life in all its fullness – had just begun.

This is conversion faith – the faith that saves. It is the kind of faith about which Paul speaks in Romans 10:9:

> If you confess with your mouth, 'Jesus is Lord', and believe in your heart that God raised him from the dead, you will be saved. For it is with your heart that you believe and are justified, and it is with your mouth that you confess and are saved.

These words show that conversion faith is not merely a matter of the intellect, it is a matter of the heart. Paul stresses that it is in our heart (*kardia*) that we must believe that Jesus has been raised from the dead. Furthermore, he also emphasizes that this faith is not something purely private. It must be vocalized in the confession, 'Jesus is Lord'. Thus, true conversion faith is a faith in the crucified and risen Lord Jesus. It is a faith that is a matter of the heart as well as the mind, and it is a faith that is expressed outwardly, not just felt and experienced inwardly.

Continuing Faith

The second kind of faith mentioned in the New Testament is 'continuing faith'. Paul says that one of the fruit of the Spirit is *pistis*, which can be translated as either 'faith' or 'faithfulness' (Galatians 5:22). I prefer the second translation. Continuing, ongoing faithfulness is one sign of the work of the Spirit in our lives. Our ability to go on believing in Jesus right to the very end of our Christian lives is what I mean by 'continuing' faith. It is that resolve to 'keep right on to the end of the road', come what may. In that respect, it is interesting to note that John's gospel never uses the noun *pistis*, it only uses the verb *pisteuein*. This preference for a verb over a noun indicates that John saw faith as a dynamic, continuing phenomenon, not something static and unchanging. This is further indicated by John's use of the present continuous tense when he talks about 'believing':

> God so loved the world that he gave his one and only Son, that whoever *goes on believing in him* shall not perish but have everlasting life (John 3:16).
>
> These things have been written that you may *go on believing* that Jesus is the Christ, the Son of God ...
>
> (John 20:31)

'Continuing faith' is therefore that ability to go on believing throughout our Christian lives. If conversion faith starts us on the way, then continuing faith helps us to walk it faithfully, and indeed to come to that destination where we can hear the words of Jesus, 'Well done, my good and *faithful* servant'. Thus 'continuing' faith is as vital as 'conversion' faith. This is because salvation has a past, present and future dimension to it, according to the New Testament. I was saved in the past when, at the age of seventeen, I confessed my faith in Jesus. I continue to be saved in the present, as I continue in my belief in Jesus. I will be saved in the future, if I end my life still trusting and obeying the Lord Jesus Christ. The following illustration highlights this past, present and future dimension of salvation very well:

A lifeboat once went out to a wrecked ship off Littlehampton. As it left the side of the sinking vessel, a woman sitting in it said, 'Thank God we are saved!' [This is past salvation – saved from the wreck.] As the boat was rowed over the sea towards the land, the saved people in the boat were still being saved. [This is present salvation – being saved in the lifeboat.] When at last the lifeboat reached the harbour at Littlehampton, a man was heard to remark, 'We are landed safely.' [This is future salvation – freedom from the very sea itself.][2]

The reason why 'continuing' faith is vital is simply because we cannot complacently rely for our salvation on a past confession of faith in Jesus Christ. We must go on believing, as John's gospel insists. What then, are the hallmarks of continuing faith? Hebrews 11:1–2 gives the answer:

Now faith is being sure of what we hope for and certain of what we do not see. This is what the ancients were commended for.

In the rest of the chapter, the writer then gives examples of people who went on believing in what they could not yet see: Abel, Enoch, Noah, Abraham, Jacob, Joseph, Moses, Rahab. He also mentions others in passing. From the examples of these men and women, we discover the following characteristics of what I am calling 'continuing' faith:

I. FAITH IS BELIEVING EVEN WHEN I CAN'T SEE IT

This is the point made in Hebrews 11:1. Faith is being certain about what we cannot see. The world says, 'I'll believe it when I see it.' The Church says, 'I'll see it when I believe it.' Thus continuing faith means a lifelong process of believing what we cannot see. Primarily this refers to the Lord Jesus Christ. We cannot, of course, see him visibly. But we go on believing that he is real, that he is risen, and that he is returning, even though we cannot see him. That is why Jesus gives the following beatitude to Thomas, 'Blessed are those who have not seen and yet have believed.' Jesus applauds those who go on believing in him even though they cannot see him, and he also assures them that their continuing faith will be rewarded; one day they will see him face to face. The Lord therefore rewards those who continue to believe in those things which they cannot see. People like Abraham are singled out in Hebrews 11 as examples of this principle. He began a journey in faith, not knowing where he was going (11:8).

2. FAITH IS OBEYING EVEN WHEN I DON'T UNDERSTAND IT

Abraham cannot have understood why God was calling him to sacrifice his one and only son, Isaac. After all, God had promised Abraham that he would be the father of many nations. When the elderly Abraham has his first child, God asks him to sacrifice Isaac. At the human level, this makes absolutely no sense at all. Yet Abraham obeyed, even though he cannot have understood why he was being asked to do it. That is a true sign of 'continuing' faith. The person who continues to exercise faith throughout their life is a person who goes on obeying God, even when the call seems incomprehensible.

3. FAITH IS PERSEVERING EVEN WHEN I DON'T FEEL LIKE IT

Again, this is a characteristic of 'continuing' faith – what Calvinists call 'the perseverance of the saints'. In Hebrews 11, men like Abraham and Moses persevered to the very end of their lives, even though there must have been times when they felt like giving up. This is specifically said of Moses in Hebrews 11:27: 'he persevered because he saw him who is invisible.' The person who 'goes on believing' is the one who goes on persevering in the direction God has called, even when the way back to Egypt seems far more desirable (Hebrews 11:26).

4. FAITH IS TRUSTING EVEN WHEN I DON'T RECEIVE IT ALL

The one whose life is marked by continuing faith goes on believing even though God's promises are not fulfilled in that person's lifetime. Moses, after all, kept on trusting in God's promise concerning the Promised Land, even though he never entered it himself. In Hebrews 11:39, the writer says that all the heroes mentioned in that chapter were commended for their faith, 'yet none of them received what had been promised'. 'What had been promised' was the Messiah, Jesus, yet none of the ancients were alive when he came to earth. They are therefore applauded for continuing to trust in God, even though they never saw the complete fulfilment of God's promise.

'Continuing' faith is therefore essential for our salvation. Jesus taught that 'he who stands firm to the end will be saved' (Matthew 10:22; 24:13). We must keep pressing on with continuing faith if we are to be saved on the Last Day. For this reason, the writer to the Hebrews says, 'Without faith it is impossible to please God' (11:6). Without that continuing faithfulness which is the true sign of discipleship, we cannot receive God's favour, acceptance and blessing. We cannot please God.

When I think of this kind of faith, I think of a man in my church called Arthur Smith. When I arrived as vicar, he was in his early sixties. He had been serving the Lord in that church all his life, and was a tremendous blessing to the Body of Christ. He was always the first to climb up ladders and mend parts of the building. He also had a tremendous love for all the people, whether long time worshippers or newly arrived. In short, he was an ordinary man with an extraordinary gift of service. A couple of years after I began my ministry there, Arthur was diagnosed as having terminal cancer. The Lord made it clear through a number of prophetic words that this sickness would not be healed. In the last month of his life, I therefore visited Arthur and asked him what he wanted to be said and sung at his funeral. He asked me to share that 'true faith is golden in the sight of God', and he asked for the hymn, 'Great is thy Faithfulness'. When Arthur's funeral came, it was a time of great sadness but it was also a time of great celebration – a celebration of one who had discovered the secret of continuing faith in the Lord Jesus Christ. The reading which Arthur requested really says it all:

In this hope you greatly rejoice, though now for a little while you may have had to suffer grief in all kinds of trials. These have come so that your faith – of greater worth than gold, which perishes even though refined by fire – may be proved genuine and may result in praise, glory and honour when Jesus Christ is revealed. Though you have not seen him, you love him; even though you do not see him now, you believe in him and are filled with an inexpressible and glorious joy, for you are receiving the goal of your faith, the salvation of your souls.

(1 Peter 1:6–9)

Charismatic Faith

All 3 types are gifts

When Paul speaks of the 'gift of faith', he does not mean 'conversion faith', nor 'continuing faith', but 'charismatic faith'. All three are the work of the Spirit. Conversion faith, writes Paul, is not something which comes from within ourselves, but is 'a gift (*doron*) from God' (Ephesians 2:8). Continuing faith, writes Paul, is a fruit of the Holy Spirit (Galatians 5:23), not something which we manufacture in our own strength. Similarly, the gift of faith is a charismatic endowment. It is an anointing given to some members of the Body of Christ in a special time of need. It is the spontaneous assurance that God is going to work in power and remove some great mountain of impossibility.

Since the earliest days of Pentecostalism, this special gift of faith has been experienced, appreciated and exercised. One of the Pentecostal pioneers whose life seems to have been saturated with this particular gift was the Bradford plumber Smith Wigglesworth. He had an extraordinary ministry as a healing evangelist, and is said to have raised fourteen people from the dead during the course of his life. His motto was, 'It is when we believe that something happens.' In one of his many sermons on faith, Wigglesworth preached on Hebrews 11 and stated, 'There is only one way to all the treasures of God, and that is *the way of faith.*' He then cited an example of such faith in his own ministry. He told the story of a young woman who was beyond all medical help. When Wigglesworth arrived at her house she was in a state of uncontrollable frenzy. However, Wigglesworth did not focus on these symptoms; he lifted his eyes to the heavens and prayed. This is how he describes what happened next:

I saw there, in the presence of that demented girl, limitations to my faith; but as I prayed there came another faith into my heart that could not be denied, a faith that grasped the promises, a faith that

> believed God's Word. I came from the presence of the glory back to
> earth. I was not the same man. I confronted the same conditions I had
> seen before, but this time it was in the name of Jesus. With a faith that
> could shake hell and move anything else, I cried to the demon power
> that was making this young woman a maniac, 'Come out of her, in the
> name of Jesus!' She rolled over and fell asleep, and awakened in four-
> teen hours, perfectly sane and perfectly whole.[3]

What Wigglesworth received as he prayed was the gift of faith. That
gift, as I wrote earlier, is associated particularly with the gifts of
healing and miraculous works. In this case, charismatic faith was
ministered to Wigglesworth so that he could heal a young woman
who was beyond medical help, and then restore her to her husband
and young child. The gift of faith, accordingly, is an essential
endowment in the Body of Christ today. There are many challenges
which lie in front of any church that desires to move on with God.
Mountains of financial, relational, spiritual, and other impossibilities
will loom large at some stage or another. How are we going to tack-
le these obstacles when they come? Are we going to seek to overcome them in our own strength? Or are we going to look to the
heavens and pray for the gift of faith? The lessons of both Scripture
and church history teach us that there is only one way: we must pray
for the gift of mountain-moving faith. Faith is the key. As Smith
Wigglesworth put it, in the final sentence of the sermon just cited:

> Have faith in God, have faith in the Son, have faith in the Holy Spirit;
> and the Triune God will work in you, working in you to will and to do
> all the good pleasure of his will.[4]

The Faith Movement

When Jesus taught his disciples about faith in Mark 11:22–25, he
was teaching them about 'charismatic faith'. When they asked him
how he had caused the fig-tree to wither, Jesus replied, 'Have faith
in God'. In Pauline language, Jesus is asking his disciples to operate
in 'the gift of faith' – the charismatic faith in the God who can level

mountains (Isaiah 45:2). Jesus then teaches about the power of this kind of faith. He says that if anyone tells a mountain to throw itself into the sea, and does so 'in faith', then it will do so. Provided that the person has no doubt in his heart, and really believes that it is going to happen, then the impossible will occur. That means operating with what Wigglesworth, in the story above, called 'a faith that could shake hell and move anything else' – a faith that can only be had through the Holy Spirit. Jesus tells his disciples that the key to praying with such faith is to ask, believing that we have already had the prayer answered! Provided that our relationships with others are not polluted by bitterness, then mighty things will occur. Unforgiveness blocks the free flow of God's wonder-working power. Therefore, Jesus concludes this passage by insisting, 'When you stand praying, if you hold anything against anyone, forgive him' (Mark 11:25).

The reader may be aware that the so-called Faith Movement has taken hold of this Scripture and created a whole theology and technology of dynamic, mountain-moving faith out of it. The basic thesis of the Faith teachers is that faith is a force-field of power which is released as we speak out in faith. The key thing is to 'name it and claim it', with particular reference to health and wealth. This is not the place for a full-blown critique of Faith teaching, so I will only voice a few concerns below:

1. The Faith Movement claims that all Christians are meant to operate in dynamic, mountain-moving faith. This is biblically unsound, not to mention pastorally divisive. Mountain-moving faith is a gift given to some but not to all. The basic mistake made by the Faith teachers is that they confuse 'charismatic' faith with 'continuing' faith. They argue that *all* Christians are supposed to operate with mountain-moving faith *all* the time. I see no evidence for this in Scripture. The kind of faith which all Christians are supposed to exhibit is 'continuing faith'. Charismatic faith, on the other hand, is to be exhibited by *some* Christians *some* of the time – like other gifts of the Spirit.

2. Jesus says, 'Have faith in God.' It is supremely important to remember that our faith is in God, not in faith itself. Some of the Faith teachers have deified the gift of faith, turning it into an object

of devotion. However, this is dangerous for two reasons. First, we are called to worship God, not the processes of dynamic believing. Secondly, the elevation of one spiritual gift over all the others is precisely the mistake which Paul sought to rectify in 1 Corinthians. In Corinth, an élitist group of super-charismatics had elevated the gift of tongues and were using that as the bench-mark of a higher spirituality. In the Faith Movement today, what we have is simply a variant form of this mistake. Instead of tongues, the Faith teachers have elevated the gift of faith.

3. The Faith teachers emphasize the importance of positive confession. They urge people to understand the link between confession and possession. As they confess in faith their need for health and wealth, so they will possess it. Quite apart from the somewhat sinister connotations of 'magic' (making speech the agent of spiritual power), this view is totally untenable. It is simply not biblical to say that God intends all of us to have all the things we want, including material prosperity. God intends us to have those things that are consistent with his will. As one of my friends has put it:

> You can have faith the size of a mustard seed, and if it's God's will, you'll be able to move a mountain.
>
> You can also have faith the size of a mountain, but if it isn't God's will, you'll not be able to move a mustard seed!

That is surely right. God intends us to live simple lifestyles, not lifestyles of luxury. Put another way, the Christian Gospel is more an 'Austerity Gospel' than a 'Prosperity Gospel'. While it is right to pray for healing when we are sick, and for material blessings when we are in a time of genuine need, we must be careful to ask in accordance with God's will, and also with the right motives (James 4:3).

So there are very real problems with the Faith Movement. On the one hand we can be grateful to the Faith teachers for reminding the Church of its desperate need for charismatic faith. On the other hand, we need to correct them for confusing charismatic faith with continuing faith, and for using charismatic faith in a quasi-magical and materialistic way. For this reason I agree entirely with the assessment of Rod Williams:

The word-of-faith teaching, all in all, is man-centred and not God-centred. This has been evidenced in such errors as believing that we can put God to work for us and that our lips can make us paupers or millionaires. Both faith and confession tend to assume divine prerogatives; that is, they create realities. A positive confession is seen to be a sure ticket to health and prosperity because the confession itself brings about the possession. Such a viewpoint, prevalent also in much so-called positive thinking today, is basically self-oriented and ultimately makes our words (not God's Word) the power behind successful living ... What is needed in this teaching is a deeper stress on faith as God's gift – as a gift of the Holy Spirit – and on the fact that he apportions faith as he wills.[5]

The Art of Prevailing Prayer

After this rather negative critique, it is important to end on a constructive note. In particular, it is vital for us to understand how the gift of faith can be used in a biblical, authentic and edifying way. One of the best examples of how to use 'charismatic faith' is surely that of George Muller. Muller felt called by God to set up orphanages in Bristol, even though he had few resources with which to achieve this goal. He simply believed and obeyed the words of Jesus, 'Have faith in God'. At the height of his ministry, he ran seven day-schools which were attended by 80,000 children. In just one of the orphanages which he established, over 10,000 children were given shelter and a home. Muller ran this entire work by faith. On many days there was no money, no milk and no food. However, God gave him special faith for all these basic needs. Some days, unexpected provisions would turn up at the door even as he was praying, 'Give us this day our daily bread'. At other times, nothing came, but the Lord miraculously kept the children from feeling hungry (on one occasion for as long as two weeks).

George Muller did not see himself as special, so he was reluctant to call this kind of faith 'charismatic' or special. However, there can be little doubt that Muller was in fact anointed with this particular gift. Muller was a man who was empowered by the Holy Spirit to believe that great mountains of impossibility would be levelled before him – mountains of money, food, shelter, help and strength. By looking to the Lord Jesus Christ, believing in the promises of God's Word, asking in accordance with God's will, and persevering in prayer, Muller prevailed in the work to which he was called. George Muller's life is therefore a wonderful testimony to the way in which charismatic faith can move mountains. John Chrysostom once described the gift of faith as 'the mother of miracles'. Cyril of Jerusalem called it 'that faith which effects things beyond man's power'.[6] Ordinary people like George Muller and Smith Wigglesworth were enabled to do extraordinary things for God on account of this gift. As Rod Williams says,

> This manifestation of the Holy Spirit, the gift of faith, needs earnestly to be sought, recognized and utilized, so that the community of believers may receive fuller ministry and God may be all the more glorified.[7]

Questions

1 Have you ever experienced what I have called 'conversion' faith?
2 In terms of 'continuing' faith, are you pressing on with the Lord in an attitude of trust, obedience and perseverance?
3 Have you ever experienced a surge of confidence that God is going to work in tremendous power?
4 Are there any 'mountains' of impossibility in your life right now?
5 What are the things for which your church needs 'charismatic faith'?
6 Have you seen a close connection between the gift of faith and the gifts of healing and miraculous works?
7 Is it right to believe that God will give us everything we want?

Prayer

Lord Jesus Christ, I thank you for the gift of faith. I thank you that the Holy Spirit distributes all the gifts within the Body of Christ. I thank you for those times in my own life when I now recognize that this gift has been at work. I ask today that you would sovereignly bestow this gift upon the leaders of your Church, that they move forward in divine confidence, knowing that nothing can stop the Holy Spirit of God. For those leaders who, like Zerubbabel, are discouraged, I ask that you would grant them 'charismatic' faith. And for those in the Church who are facing mountains of difficulty, I ask that you would give them a surge of supernatural confidence in the God who provides and heals. In your name I ask. Amen.

FOUR

The Gifts of Healing

We come now to the fourth gift in the list in 1 Corinthians 12:8-10, 'the gifts of healings'. This is the only gift which is prefaced by the word *charismata*. In Greek the phrase is *charismata hiamaton*, which literally means 'grace-gifts of healings'. It is difficult to be certain why Paul did not simply write, 'healing'. After all, he has not found it necessary to put *charismata* before any of the other gifts of the Spirit. However, we may speculate that in Corinth there was a tendency for those with healing gifts to be 'pedestalized' by others. In other words, those who had a proven track record in praying for the sick and seeing them supernaturally cured may well have been regarded as more effective and more spiritual than others. Paul nips that view in the bud by making it very clear that 'healings' are the product of *charismata*. They are the result of the operation of God's grace, not of super-spiritual piety. Accordingly, 'healing' is a charismatic endowment not a status indicator. It is yet another example of the unmerited love of God – in this case directed at both the one who uses the gifts of healing, and the ones who are healed.

The second interesting thing to note about Paul's description of this gift is the fact that he has healing in the plural; he speaks of 'gifts of healings' not 'the gift of healing'. This implies that Paul envisages a diversity of healing phenomena. Some people claim that Paul is thinking of different kinds of healing ministry. They think that 'healing' is in the plural because healing can take a variety of forms: deliverance, the healing of emotional or mental disorders, physical cures, and so on. This diversity, they argue, prevents any one healing ministry from 'cornering the market', as it were. They further claim that Paul wants to humble those who think that they are the only ones with healing gifts by showing that there are others around with a related anointing. He does this by talking about 'gifts of healings' rather than 'the gift of healing'. However, in response to this idea, we do need to notice that Paul does not say,

'to others [are given] gifts of healings,'

he says,

'to another [is given] gifts of healings.'

one person with a variety of healing ministries

Paul is therefore talking about the different kinds of healing gifts that one person can exercise, not the different kinds of healing ministries which arise within the Church. Paul is basically saying that the person who is charismatically endowed with healing gifts will have a varied ministry. On one occasion they may find themselves liberating someone who is oppressed by demonic spirits. On another they may find themselves being used by God to bring healing from physical illness. On yet another they may find themselves being empowered by the Lord to bring wholeness to someone who is mentally and emotionally traumatized. On other occasions they may be used to effect immediate healing in a broken relationship. The healing gifts which can be used by a believer are therefore very varied. Indeed, they are probably as diverse as the illnesses which are confronted.

A number of further points need to be made. First of all, like all the gifts of the Spirit, 'healings' are given to some believers but not to all. Thus we find Paul asking, 'Do all have gifts of healings?' (1 Corinthians 12:29). The answer to the question is 'no'. This does not mean that those who do not have the healing gifts will never operate in this particular anointing. Far from it! I do believe that it is perfectly right for those of us who have other gifts to ask for the gifts of healing on those occasions when the need arises. I also believe that the teaching of James 5:13–16 encourages every church leadership team to have faith for healing when they are called out to pray for the sick. But the more typical situation in Paul's mind is this: that there are some members of the Body of Christ who are given the special ability to minister healing on a regular basis. For Paul, then, 'gifts of healings' are just one of the manifestations of the Spirit. They are not given to everyone, they are given 'to each one' as the Holy Spirit determines.

Secondly, Paul does not see the healing gifts as a temporary endowment. This is borne out by his use of the verb 'to have' in 1 Corinthians 12:29:

'Do all have (*exousin*) gifts of healings?'

The verb 'to have' is in the present continuous tense here. An accurate rendition might therefore be, 'Do all continue to have gifts of healings?' The implied answer to the question is, 'No, but some believers do have these gifts as an ongoing anointing'. Consequently, if healings are your particular gift, then you should expect to minister in this way on a consistent basis. Like all the gifts, 'healings' are therefore supposed to be understood as a long-term rather than an occasional enabling in the believer's life.

Thirdly, it is really important that we notice what Paul does *not* say. Paul never speaks of 'healers'. He speaks of those 'having the gifts of healing'. This is particularly evident at the end of 1 Corinthians 12:

> And in the Church God has appointed first of all apostles, second prophets, third teachers, then works of miracles, then gifts of healings, helpful deeds, governings, different kinds of tongues.
>
> (1 Corinthians 12:28)

The first three in this list – apostles, prophets and teachers – are ministries or offices. The next five are gifts of the Spirit – miracles, gifts of healing, helps, governings, different kinds of tongues. This switch from 'offices' to 'gifts' is significant because it shows that Paul resisted the temptation to use the words 'healers' or 'faith healers'. He does not say,

> And in the Church God has appointed first of all apostles, secondly prophets, third teachers, fourth miracle-workers, fifth healers, sixth helpers, seventh orchestrators, and eighth tongue-speakers.

If Paul resisted the temptation to bill certain people as 'healers', then so should we. Even in Ephesians 4:11, Paul refuses to identify 'healers' in the list of charismatic ministries. There he mentions 'apostles, prophets, evangelists, pastor-teachers'. He does not mention either 'healers' or 'miracle-workers'. This shows that healing is part of the work of the Church, not the whole of it.

A fourth important reminder is this: that Paul understood this particular gift as a spiritual anointing, not as a natural talent or a learnt skill. In recent times there has been a tendency to equate modern medicine with what Paul meant by healing. There is no doubt in my mind that God works through many aspects of the medical profession to bring healing to sick people. However, Paul understood 'healings' as *charismata*. As Rod Williams has put it:

> Gifts of healings are wholly supernatural endowments. They are not natural gifts, nor are they the result of developed skills. The word 'gifts', *charismata*, emphasizes their continuing divine origin and character. They come directly from the exalted Lord. Where he is recognized and received as Lord ('Jesus is Lord' [1 Corinthians 12:3]), he freely moves through a particular person to bring about healings.[1]

While we need to take care not to create an inseparable dualism between nature and grace, it is imperative that we understand Paul's intent in relation to the healing gifts. Whether we like it or not, he was not talking about the NHS. He was talking about a divine enabling.

Fifthly, it is often said that the healing gifts are only effective in relation to psychosomatic disorders. Thus, James Dunn proposes that Jesus' healings were in fact exclusively and solely psychosomatic in nature. He writes:

No doubt Jesus was responsible for curing mental illness, blindness, lameness and deafness; but these could all be hysterical disorders ... There is no instance of a healing miracle which falls clearly outside the general category of psychosomatic illnesses.[2]

Now it is important to be fair to Dunn at this point. In the context of his overall argument, Dunn is saying that there are no examples of the healing of purely physical injuries in what he calls the earliest stratum of Jesus tradition. In other words, he is saying that the descriptions of Jesus performing physical (i.e. non-psychosomatic) diseases derive from the evangelists. The stories of healings which are psychosomatic in nature are more likely to have actually happened. My own view is that this is mistaken. Matthew says that Jesus healed EVERY disease and EVERY infirmity (Matthew 4:23; 9:35). In the same way, Matthew writes that Jesus sent out the apostles to heal EVERY disease and EVERY infirmity (Matthew 10:1). I am therefore unwilling to limit 'healing gifts' to purely psychosomatic disorders, either in the ministry of Jesus or the ministry of the Church. Apart from anything else, that would not only involve restricting Paul's understanding of 'healing'. It would also mean calling Matthew a liar.

Sixthly, the use of these healing gifts should not be seen as restricted to the context of the Church's worship. The context of 1 Corinthians 12:8–10 is Paul's instructions concerning charismatic worship. Chapters 11–14 are all devoted to the question of how to worship in a charismatic and yet at the same time an orderly and fitting way. Paul understands the grace-gifts of the Spirit – including healings – to be signs of the manifest presence of the Spirit in public worship. At the same time, however, we must guard against seeing all of these gifts as occurring solely within the public worship of the Church. The evidence of both the ministry of Jesus and indeed the Acts of the Apostles would compel us to conclude that the healing gifts are for the market-place as well as the worship-place. I therefore agree with Francis Martin, who writes,

There is a specific gift, possessed by some but not by others, which provides for healing both within and outside of the community and,

in both instances, witnesses to the power of the Resurrection to offset
the moral and physical consequences of individual and communal sin.[3]

Seventhly, the last point about the relationship between sin and
sickness is significant. Paul certainly took the standard Jewish line
on this, that human sickness is a consequence of human sin. Thus,
in 1 Corinthians 11:30, he mentions some who have become weak
or sick in the Corinthian church. Why? because they have been
abusing the Lord's Supper, and turning it into an opportunity for
drunken revelry. This shows that Paul saw a causal relationship
between disobedience and disease. As far as the nature of this relationship is concerned, I myself take the following view:

All sickness is *indirectly* due to sin – to 'man's first disobedience' in
the Garden of Eden, which brought sickness and death into the
world. All disease is therefore *ultimately* the result of the Fall.
 Only some sicknesses are *directly* due to sins committed by the
individuals who are ill. In those cases, repentance and absolution is
needed before healing can be released. (Mark 2:5; James 5:16)

In this respect I believe that there is an important connection
between healing and the cross. Martin, in the quotation above, talks
about healing events as evidence of the power of the Resurrection.
That is true, but they are also one of the many benefits of the cross.
The cross is the place where sin's price was paid. As such, healing
should be understood as one of the blessings of the Atonement.
The fact that healing is the only gift which Paul specifically calls a
charisma seems to confirm this. *Charisma*, as we observed in the
Introduction, has the word *charis* in it, meaning 'grace'. Healing is
therefore an operation of grace, and grace is supremely revealed at
Calvary, where the cause of sickness (human sin) was dealt with
'once and for all'.

An eighth and final reminder concerns the permanence of the
healing gifts. While the person who receives these gifts receives
them on a permanent rather than a temporary basis, the same is not
true of the Church as a whole. The healing gifts, like all the gifts,
are in operation 'until perfection comes' (1 Corinthians 13:10). In

the Introduction I interpreted that phrase as, 'until the end comes' (i.e. the return of Christ). When Jesus Christ returns, God will create a new heaven and a new earth out of the existing heaven and earth. This work of divine re-creation will result in a cosmos in which there is no more sin and no more sickness. On that day God will wipe away every tear from our eyes. There will be no more hospitals, no more morgues and no more undertakers. As such, the healing gifts will no longer be needed. So while they are required in the 'now' of the kingdom of God, they will no longer be required in the 'not yet'. In the meantime, we live inbetween the times, and during these 'last days' the healing gifts are very necessary.

With those eight points in mind, we can now summarize our findings. Accordingly, the definition which I would like to offer of these healing gifts is as follows:

> *the healing gifts are best understood as the special, charismatic ability to heal illnesses in the power of the Holy Spirit, and through faith in Jesus Christ. This ability is given to some people in the Body of Christ, and they are expected to use this gift faithfully and continuously until the Lord Jesus returns and does away with sickness for ever.*

Seen in this light, the healing gifts are important for the Church's life, worship and mission. They are presents which are well worth unwrapping and well worth using, for the glorification of Christ and the edification of the Church.

The Practice of Healing

In a chapter of this length it would be impossible to provide a comprehensive guide to the use of the healing gifts. Whole books have already been devoted to this subject, and there are useful chapters on it in books like *Come, Holy Spirit* (David Pytches). Having said that, this chapter does give me an opportunity to address an issue which I have not yet tackled. This concerns the ways in which the different gifts in 1 Corinthians 12:8–10 relate to each other. Clearly, in the case of tongues and interpretation of tongues, there is a very obvious connection between the two gifts. As we will see in the final chapters, Paul says that a public tongue must be interpreted. This highlights the limitation of public tongue-speaking without the companion gift of interpretation. Likewise, the gift of prophecy seems to be paired with the 'discernings of spirits'. The implication is that we need the latter if we are to correctly interpret and apply the former. Indeed, prophecy, like tongues, has only limited value if there is no weighing and evaluating of the supposed prophetic utterances. What, then, of the healing gifts? What other gifts are needed for healing to be properly and effectively handled in the Church?

There are three *charismata* which are particularly vital if the healing gifts are to have their full impact on the sick. The first gift essential in this ministry is the gift of faith. I have already defined 'charismatic' faith in the last chapter, where I described it as a spontaneous surge of unshakeable confidence that God is about to act in a particularly powerful way. If genuine, immediate healing is to happen, then this kind of faith is obviously going to be required. It is going to be particularly important on the part of those who pray for the sick. Thus, when Peter and John have healed the man at the Gate Beautiful in Acts 3, they are particularly insistent about the role of faith in the healing process:

> By faith in the name of Jesus, this man whom you see and know, was made strong. It is Jesus' name, and the faith that comes through him, that has given this healing to him, as you can all see.
>
> (Acts 3:16)

So for Peter and John, the key to the man's healing was faith. In this instance they are not referring to 'conversion' or 'continuing' faith but to 'charismatic' faith, i.e. the gift of faith. This is confirmed by the way in which they pray for the man in the first place. Peter says,

> I have no silver or gold, but what I have I give you. In the name of Jesus Christ of Nazareth, walk.

Such words of authority are only possible when the Spirit has ministered unshakeable confidence to a person's heart. This is precisely what happened in Peter's case.

One of the gifts which has to be used in conjunction with the healing gifts is therefore the gift of faith. As Rod Williams has put it:

> The gift of faith ... may be the immediate background for the exercise of the two ministry gifts that follow; gifts of healing and effecting of miracles. Faith is the atmosphere in which healings occur; it is likewise the basic precondition for the working of miracles ... Faith, while seemingly passive, is the crucial factor in these ensuing gifts.[4]

James Dunn says much the same thing in relation to Jesus' ministry:

> It was characteristic of Jesus therefore that he looked for faith in those to whom he ministered. Faith was the necessary complement to the exercise of God's power through him, hence his inability to perform any mighty work in Nazareth because of their lack of faith (*apistia* – Mark 6:6; Matthew 13:58). Faith ... completed the circuit so that the power could flow.[5]

Now let us ask what it is that we are actually believing in when we exercise this kind of faith. We are believing in the name of Jesus Christ, and in the promises of Scripture. That much is self-evident. But we are also believing in something else; that the power of God is present to heal in a particular situation. In this respect, it has always felt highly significant to me that Luke reports the following detail just prior to one of Jesus' most dramatic healings:

> And the power of the Lord was present for Jesus to heal the sick.
> (Luke 5:17)

The implication of this statement is that there are times when God's healing power is present, and there are times when it is not. The gift which enables us to sense that presence is 'discernment' and the gift which enables us to act on that discernment is 'faith'. The gift of faith is therefore released when God gives us a consciousness of his power. As the following testimony reveals, it is charismatic faith which intuits God's healing presence. The writer in the following paragraph is a Bible scholar called Samuel Storms:

One Sunday a couple came to me before the service and asked the elders of our church to anoint their infant son and pray for his healing. After the service we gathered in the back room and I anointed him with oil. I do not recall the precise medical name for his condition, but at six months of age he had a serious liver disorder that would require immediate surgery, possibly even a transplant, if something did not change. As we prayed, something unusual happened. As we laid hands on this young child, I found myself suddenly filled with an overwhelming and inescapable confidence that he would be healed. It was altogether unexpected. I recall actually trying to doubt, but could not. I prayed confidently, filled with a faith unshakeable and undeniable. I said to myself, 'Lord, you really are going to heal him'. Although the family left the room unsure, I was absolutely *certain* God had healed him. The next morning the doctor agreed. He was totally healed and is a healthy, happy young boy today.[6]

In this testimony the author is talking not just about the healing gifts but about the gift of faith. He says that he was filled with 'an overwhelming and inescapable confidence that he would be healed'. He writes that he was filled 'with a faith unshakeable and undeniable'. The use of the passive verb 'filled' shows that the writer is speaking of a force that he was given, rather than an attitude which he himself summoned up. In short, we are talking about a manifestation of the Spirit here: the gift of faith.

If healing gifts require the gift of faith they also require the gift of prophecy. We will study this particular gift more closely in chapter 6. However, at this stage I need just to mention that one of the purposes of New Testament prophecy can be summed up by the word *kardiagnosis*. The word *kardia* means 'heart' and *gnosis* means 'knowledge'. In biblical times, prophets were thought to possess the spiritual ability to know by revelation the secrets of a person's heart. This could relate to a person's hidden sins or even to a person's sicknesses. It seems to be this particular, spontaneous ability which Paul is referring to in 1 Corinthians 14:24–25, when he wrote about the use of prophecy in public worship. He considered that gift to be particularly important because it had the effect of revealing (*apokalupto*) the secrets of an unbeliever's heart, with the result that the unbeliever was convicted of his sins, fell on his face and declared, 'God is really among you!' Whenever this form of prophecy occurred, there was therefore a kind of *apokalupsis* or 'unveiling of secrets'. In this sense, an authentic prophetic utterance is an apocalyptic event.

The gift of prophecy has enormous value in the healing ministry. It is often the case that God exposes a particular disease before he heals it. This is most often a simple revelation of a person's symptoms or actual illness (with the person receiving the revelation sometimes even experiencing those symptoms). In the context of public worship, the use of this gift can often lead to quite dramatic results. The following testimony comes from the theologian Jack Deere, who went to a John Wimber conference as a sceptic. Deere was, at the time, a cessationist, believing that the miraculous gifts of the Spirit had ceased with the death of the last apostle. However, what he saw at the Wimber conference changed his perspective for good. He saw a visiting preacher speaking words of insight which could only have been revealed by the Holy Spirit. The example in question concerns a word about a woman with a longstanding back problem, whom John asks to come to the front. At first she does not come forward. So John Wimber prays for more revelation, which he then shares: 'You went to the doctor several days ago, you have had this pain for years.' The woman still does not come forward. Then John even gets the name: 'Your name is Margaret.' Finally, with a grandfatherly smile, he says, 'Now Margaret, you get up and come here right now.' Jack Deere describes what happened next:

About halfway down the centre section, next to the aisle, Margaret got up and began to walk rather sheepishly toward the front.

I thought that this was the most amazing thing I had ever seen. This was just how the apostle Paul said it should happen. There was awe and conviction in the room. But before Margaret made it down to the front of the church, a wave of scepticism and disgust came over me. I said to myself, *What if he paid her to do this. What if she's Margaret on Thursday night here in Fort Worth, Texas, and then on Saturday night in some other city she is Mabel MacClutchbut* ... And I said to myself, *I don't believe this is true.*

At about the same time I had begun to doubt this whole process, the man sitting next to me, whom I had known for fifteen years and who was also in my church exclaimed, 'That's Margaret, my sister-in-law!'

Mike Pinkston's sister-in-law, Margaret Pinkston, went down to the front of the church that evening after being called out specifically by John Wimber. And when several adults prayed for her, she was healed of a condition she had had for years. I knew that family, and I knew there was nothing fake about that healing. This was a really graphic illustration of New Testament church life as revealed by the apostle Paul in 1 Corinthians 14.[7]

The gift of prophecy, then, is vital in the healing ministry. In this particular example, John Wimber received a prophetic word concerning the nature of an illness, the gender of the person who had the illness, the fact that the illness was a longterm one, the fact that the person had just visited her doctor, and, most remarkable of all, the name of the person concerned. That is amazing by any score. What is more, it shows how essential prophecy is for an effective use of the healing gifts.

It is particularly important in relation to the whole issue of confession. The apostle James states that it is vital to confess sins to one another before prayer is made for healing. If a person is to receive healing, they must first confess any sins which might have caused the sickness (directly or indirectly) and which might therefore obstruct the healing process. It is precisely at this point that the gift of prophecy is helpful because it lays bare the secrets of people's hearts. Indeed, I well remember an occasion when I was praying for a Christian woman who had been sick for a long time. As I was praying for her, the word 'abortion' flashed into my mind. I asked if that meant anything to anyone. The husband whispered in my ear that he and his wife had had sexual intercourse before they were married. On one occasion they thought she was pregnant and had gone to the local clinic to arrange an abortion. As it turned out she was not, but the incident had haunted them ever since, and they had not confessed it to anyone. Needless to say, that night there had to be forgiveness of sins before effective healing prayer could happen. Here then is yet another example of the way the prophetic gift often accompanies the healing gifts.

A third gift which I believe is vital to the healing ministry is what Paul calls 'discernings of spirits'. At this point it is important to recognize that there are many different kinds of healing. There is physical healing (the healing of bodily diseases or injuries), emotional or inner healing (healing from the wounds of the past), spiritual healing (healing from evil spirits), relational healing (the healing of broken relationships), to name just a few. When a person is used by God to effect liberation in any of these kinds of context then she or he has been operating in the healing gifts. In all of these situations there is a great need to be able to discern the spirit at work behind a particular problem or affliction. Here is what Rod Williams says about the importance of charismatic discernment:

> The discernings of spirits is ... important in dealing with certain cases of illness. Is a particular ailment only physical or mental, or is there perhaps some demonic power at work? It is quite significant that in his ministry Jesus dealt with two situations of deafness in radically different ways. In the one case there was a man who 'was deaf and had an impediment of speech'; and in relation to the deafness Jesus placed his fingers in the man's ears saying 'Be opened' and the deaf man was healed (Mark 7:32–35). In the other case there was a convulsive boy who was deaf and dumb; Jesus helped him by saying, 'You deaf and dumb spirit, I command you, come out of him, and never enter him again', and the boy was made whole (Mark 9:25–27). The first case of deafness was physical and dealt with by a healing touch; the latter was spiritual and handled by deliverance. *Jesus discerned the difference.* Surely this is relevant today, for it is sometimes urgent to discern the root of a given illness and thus to know whether the ministry of healing or exorcizing is called for.[8]

Exactly, the value of the gift known as 'discernings of spirits' is great in the healing ministry. The charism of discernment gives a kind of X-ray perspective on a person's situation, illuminating the true spirit (negative or positive) at work in that person's life. In that respect, charismatic discernment 'provides depth perception of a spiritual problem that lies at the root of a human ailment.' This revelation does not actually solve the problem, but it does enable a person with the healing gifts to pray more discerningly. Sometimes this does mean praying for deliverance from evil spirits. This said, this is not the place to develop a full-blown apologetic for the existence of demons. All I will say is that they do exist, that they are supernatural 'powers' which are opposed to the will of God, that they do oppress Christians as well as unbelievers, and that we do come across them from time to time in the healing ministry. For further guidance in this whole area, I highly recommend Francis MacNutt's latest book, *Deliverance from Evil Spirits* (London, Hodder & Stoughton, 1996).

When God Does Not Heal

So there are 'gifts of healings' and there are gifts of the Spirit which need to be used alongside the healing gifts, particularly 'faith', 'prophecy' and 'discernings of spirits'. When these gifts are used wisely in the Church's ministry to the sick, then there is no doubt that God touches people's lives and brings healing. Having said that, it would be impossible not to end this chapter without at least some comments about those times when God does not heal those for whom we pray. The truth is that there are times when people are not healed of their sicknesses, in spite of fervent and compassionate prayer. In fact, Michael Buckley is surely right when he says,

> As we look around us in the world today we are more conscious of the vast sea of suffering rather than the small islands of healing.[9]

Part of this vast sea of suffering consists of those believers who are not healed when we pray for them. So why are our prayers for healing sometimes not answered? In the final pages of this chapter I will try to answer this question, first from our side, as it were, and then from God's.

I. OUR SIDE

There are a number of reasons why people may not be healed when we pray for them, reasons which have more to do with us than with God. There may, for example, be a lack of faith on the part of those who are praying for healing. When the disciples fail to heal a demonized boy, Jesus implies that it is due to their lack of faith. When he hears what a mess they made of their attempt to help the boy, Jesus declares, 'O unbelieving and perverse generation' (Matthew 17:16). There may, furthermore, be a general atmosphere of unbelief which inhibits healing. Mark writes that Jesus could not perform any miracles in his own town because of the unbelief of the locals (Mark 6:1–4). All he could do was lay his hands on a few sick people, who did have their health restored. So lack of faith can be a reason why people are not healed. However, we should note that this lack of faith is located in the people praying (and indeed in the local community) rather than in the person receiving prayer. This leads me to say that on no account should a person who is not healed be blamed for any lack of faith on their part.

A second reason why healing may not occur is because some hidden sin is acting as an obstacle to God's power. It is here that the teaching on healing in James' letter is particularly challenging:

> Is any one of you sick? He should call the elders of the church to pray over him and anoint him with oil in the name of the Lord. And the prayer offered in faith will make the sick person well; the Lord will raise him up. If he has sinned, he will be forgiven. Therefore confess your sins to each other and pray for each other so that you may be healed. The prayer of a righteous man is powerful and effective.
>
> (James 5:14–16)

This passage highlights the importance of confessing sin before praying for the sick. Note that the efficacy of healing prayer is not just dependent on the sick person's confession, but also on the confession of those who are doing the prayer ministry (in this case 'the elders' of the church). It is particularly important for any anger or unforgiveness to be exposed if healing is to occur. Often physical sicknesses can be caused by a deep root of bitterness. Until that is dealt with, then the 'prayer of faith' will not be possible. As Jesus said, in his teaching about 'charismatic' faith (which we briefly looked at in the last chapter): 'And whenever you stand praying, forgive, if you have anything against anyone' (Mark 11:25).

A third reason why spiritual healing sometimes does not occur is due to a wrong theology. Some people in the Christian Church have developed the view that any medical care is a sign of unbelief. In other words, if I have need of a blood transfusion and I go to the hospital, then I am not trusting the Lord – I should trust the Lord to do the healing, not doctors and nurses. This, of course, is a very dangerous and unscriptural doctrine. There are examples in the Bible of people being healed through natural, medicinal means. One well-known instance is found in 2 Kings 20, where King Hezekiah is suffering from a nasty boil. The Lord tells Isaiah that the king will be healed, and then instructs him how to treat him. So what was the treatment? Not the prayer of faith, but a poultice of figs applied to the boil. When this happened, Hezekiah recovered. This story clearly shows that God works through natural as well as supernatural means. We should therefore be prepared to accept medical care with gratitude, where that care can legitimately and effectively be given.

2. GOD'S SIDE

A first reason, from God's side, why someone may not be healed has to do with God's sovereignty. The fact of the matter is that God is sovereign. He decides whom he is going to heal and whom he is not going to heal. We may feel that there is sometimes something arbitrary about God's choice in this regard, but that is simply because of our limited, finite perspective. The truth is, God knows what he is about. He knows what is best for us and for the world. It is his plan not ours that matters. The important thing in the healing ministry is therefore to get in touch with God's sovereign will for a sick person. Like Jesus, we need to see what the Father is doing and act in accordance with that. Sometimes this will mean only one person in a crowd being healed. At other times it may mean every one in a crowd being healed. Sometimes it may mean someone being dramatically healed at death's door. At other times it will mean hearing God's word, 'this sickness is unto death'. It is not for us to question God's sovereign decisions. His Spirit distributes the *charismata* as he determines. His Spirit works for healing as he determines. It is therefore his will that must prevail, even when that will seems obscure to us.

A second reason why God sometimes does not heal people is because he has a different understanding of suffering from ours. Sometimes God allows us to experience suffering in order to teach us things that we could not, in the ordinary course of our lives, learn. It is here that I appreciate so much the Catholic Charismatic contribution to the healing ministry. While the Protestant Charismatic Renewal has tended to deny the possibility of 'redemptive suffering', the Catholic Renewal has always made room for it in its theology. Many Catholic Charismatics believe passionately in the power of God to heal the sick, and at the same time they believe in the value of some kinds of suffering. For them, some suffering can have a creative, spiritual significance. How then do you tell the difference between positive and negative suffering? Catholics argue that any suffering which prevents a believer from living a fully human Christian life can and should be healed – that is negative, destructive suffering. On the other hand, suffering which develops character (particularly sensitivity towards others), which enables people to love and to grow, may remain in a believer's life. Thus, suffering is positive:

1 When it is creative and helps us to grow as human beings.
2 When it allows us to experience a more profound, more intimate relationship with the Father.
3 When it enables us to enter more deeply into 'the fellowship of Christ's sufferings'.
4 When it increases our compassion for others who suffer.
5 When it causes us to live in greater trust and dependence on God.
6 When we discern, with others' help, that it is the will of God.

Seen in this light, we can understand Michael Buckley's lament: 'The tragedy is not that there is suffering in the world but that we waste it so foolishly.'[10]

A third reason why people are sometimes not healed has to do with the kingdom of God. Biblical scholars now by and large agree that Jesus spoke about the kingdom in both a realized and a futuristic sense. In his earthly ministry, Jesus understood his mighty works as evidence of the kingdom or the rule of God. For him, the raising of the dead, the healing of the sick, the deliverance of the demonized were all signs that the kingdom was irrupting into history. However, during this ministry, the dynamic rule of God was only partially inaugurated. It will not be until the *parousia* or the Second Coming of Christ that the works of the evil one will be finally and totally eradicated – works which consist of sin, sickness, suffering and death. What this therefore means is that we live 'inbetween the times', between the already and the not yet of the kingdom. In God's tomorrow, all faithful believers will experience complete healing. In God's today, however, believers still get sick, and all believers of course die (even those who are temporarily raised from death). What this means in relation to the healing ministry is this: sometimes God allows us to borrow from tomorrow. In other words, he allows us to experience today what we are in any case going to experience in the eschatological Tomorrow. Sometimes God therefore says 'Yes, Now', when we pray for healing. On other occasions God does not. In those instances, however, we should not understand his answer as a blunt and careless 'No', but as a bright and hopeful,

'Yes, but Not Yet.'

It is God who decides, not us. He is the divine potter, we are merely human clay. It is not our place to question the good and perfect will of God, even when we feel that this will is a 'mystery'.

So, to sum up, Paul speaks of gifts of healing in his list of the *charismata* in 1 Corinthians 12:8–10. God has therefore very graciously provided the means by which the sick may be healed in the Church. We may feel that some Scriptures give us a mandate for believing that all will be healed. James 5:14–16 leads us in that direction, until we recognize that the overall context of that passage is 'patience in suffering' (the suffering we will all experience 'until the Lord's coming'). The correct position, in my opinion, is that we should faithfully and consistently pray for the sick, asking God to give today what he intends to give tomorrow. Sometimes he will say, 'Yes, Now'. At other times he will reply, 'Yes, but Not Yet'. Whatever the answer and whatever the outcome, those in the Body of Christ who are endowed with healing gifts should be recognized and released to pray for the sick alongside the 'elders' of the local church. When this occurs, the group praying should ask God for faith, prophecy and discernings of spirits, so that the ministry can be both 'righteous and effective' (James 5:16). They should pray for God to release the healing of the cross and to manifest the power of the Resurrection. Most of all, they should pray, 'Your kingdom come, your will be done, on earth, as it is in heaven.'

Questions

1 Have you ever seen anyone healed as a direct answer to your prayers?
2 Do you have people with healing gifts in your church?
3 What is the practice of healing in your church?
4 Has there been a situation when faithful prayer for a sick person resulted in them deteriorating or even dying?
5 If so, how was this dealt with in terms of teaching and pastoral care?
6 What improvements, if any, do you think need to be made to the theology and practice of healing as a result of reading this chapter?

Prayer[11]

Jesus, your coming on earth was like a new dawn over a world of darkness: the blind saw, the lame walked again, the sick were healed and even the dead were raised to life. Come again into the lives of everyone and heal the wounds of their broken hearts. Come again to all who are sick or depressed and fill their lives with hope and peace. Come again to us as we call on your holy name so that we too may receive your help and healing grace. Amen.

FIVE

The Gift of Miraculous Works

We come now to the spiritual gift which, more than any other, evokes extremes of strong emotion. At one end of the spectrum are those who advertise their meetings with the most unbridled kind of hype, showing photographs of discarded crutches and wheelchairs, and making claims for great healing miracles at the hands of some well-known minister. At the other end of the spectrum are those who insist that miracles never happen, that there is no scientific evidence for the miracles which have been claimed, and that we should not encourage any teaching which implies that the miraculous is part and parcel of the Christian life today. It is therefore especially important that we start with what the New Testament has to say about this particular gift, and then develop a responsible perspective on 'miraculous works' from this biblical starting point. That way we can nurture a theology of 'miracles' which steers carefully between the Scylla of scientific materialism on one side, and the Charybdis of irrational experientialism on the other.

Healing and Miracles

If we look again at Paul's list of the *charismata*, we will see that 'miraculous works' comes straight after 'gifts of healing'. Here is the list in its entirety:

word of wisdom
word of knowledge
faith
gifts of healing
miraculous works
prophecy
discernings of spirits
kinds of tongues
interpretation of tongues

In this catalogue of some of the many 'grace-gifts', Paul seems to have several pairs of gifts. For example, the word of wisdom seems to relate closely to the word of knowledge. We might call these two gifts 'teaching *charismata*', since in both cases their purpose is to highlight something of God's plan and God's ways in both broad and specific contexts. The gifts of prophecy and discernings of spirits seem to go together, with discernment being the means by which true prophecy is distinguished from false prophecy. Interpretation of tongues and tongues obviously relate to one another, the former being necessary to translate the latter in the context of public worship. What then, of the remaining triad of gifts: faith, healings, and miraculous works? What is the relationship, if any, between these *charismata*? If wisdom and knowledge are gifts of teaching, prophecy and discernment gifts of revelation, and tongues and interpretation gifts of adoration, what are these other three?

Let us begin by reminding ourselves of what Paul meant by 'the gift of faith'. In chapter 3, I defined this *charisma* as,

> *a supernatural certainty given by the Holy Spirit to some members of the Body of Christ. This certainty is an unshakeable confidence that God is about to resolve a seemingly impossible situation, for the edification of the Church.*

In chapter 4, I pointed out that this particular gift is crucial in connection with the exercise of the healing gifts. The latter I defined in the following way:

The healing gifts are best understood as the special, supernatural ability to heal illnesses in the power of the Holy Spirit, and through faith in Jesus Christ. This ability is given to some in the Body of Christ, and they are expected to use this gift faithfully and continuously.

The importance of charismatic faith in relation to charismatic healing lies in this: that it is the exercise of faith which so often leads to the exercise of healing. It is as a person receives a special, God-given confidence in the healing presence of Jesus that supernatural cures are effected – whether those cures are to do with mental, spiritual, emotional or physical afflictions. Charismatic faith is therefore intimately connected with charismatic healing.

As far as 'miraculous works' are concerned, we can very quickly see that there is likewise a close relationship with faith. The phrase 'miraculous works' is a translation of the two Greek words, *energemata dunameōn*. The word *energemata* literally means 'workings'. It is the same word which Paul uses in 1 Corinthians 12:6:

There are different kinds of working (*energemata*), but
the same God works (*energon*) all of them in all people.

In this context, the word *energemata* is a synonym for *charismata* ('grace-gifts', 1 Corinthians 12:4) and *diakoniai* (acts of service, 12:5). The only difference lies in the notion of 'energy' or power implicit in the word. In the case of the gift of 'miraculous works', this note of 'power' is given even stronger emphasis by virtue of the addition of *dumameōn*. This is the genitive plural of *dunameis*, meaning 'mighty acts'. The gift of *energemata dunameōn* is therefore yet another example of Paul's use of the double plural. It literally means 'workings of powers', and the use of the plural in both nouns indicates that there is a certain variety in these operations. We may therefore define this gift as;

the special ability to perform acts of extraordinary supernatural power. These actions are performed through the power of the Holy Spirit and in the name of Jesus Christ, and they evoke wonder in many, and faith in some.

What, then, is the difference between 'healings' and 'miraculous works'? Surely every instance of healing is, in a sense, a miracle? My own view on this is that Paul understands 'miraculous works' as public demonstrations of extraordinary, charismatic power, and that he saw these demonstrations as taking a number of forms. As in the ministry of Jesus, there are first of all resurrection miracles. On three occasions, Jesus is said to have raised a dead person to life: Jairus' daughter, the son of the widow of Nain, and Lazarus. These were not permanent resurrections from death because each of the people in question would one day have to die again. But they were dramatic, extraordinary resurrection miracles even so. There are secondly nature miracles. Jesus transformed water into wine. He multiplied loaves and fishes. He stilled the storm. In each of these instances, Jesus performed an extraordinary act of supernatural power which radically transformed some aspect of nature. Thirdly there are the healing miracles. These were charismatic acts of power in which sick people were immediately healed of serious physical, mental and/or demonic affliction. Thus in every case – resurrection, nature and healing miracles – the common denominators are:

they were public
they were immediate
they were dramatic
they evoked wonder and awe
they involved radical transformation.

It follows from this that not all healing events can be classified as 'miraculous works'. In a truly charismatic, Christian church, all sorts of healing are going on all of the time. There is the general healing known as 'salvation'. This occurs when people give their lives to Jesus Christ and are born again of the Spirit. Then there is relational healing – people with apparently irreconcilable differences coming together in a spirit of mutual forgiveness and acceptance. Then there is what I call 'low-key' physical healing – the gradual healing of bodily disease during a period of concentrated prayer ministry. There is psychological healing – the healing of low self-worth, of past wounds, of traumas, abuse and addiction. There is spiritual healing – deliverance from demonic spirits. There is communal healing – whole churches experiencing a fresh outpouring of the love of God so that past obstacles to growth can be laid aside. There is social healing – when the poor are given life-giving resources and the oppressed are given liberty. In all these ways, and many more, healing can happen in the Church. None of these events are necessarily 'miraculous works'. They are more likely to be less visible, less immediate, less dramatic but none the less real. As such, the differences between healings and miracles can be understood in terms of 'degrees of charismatic power'. While healings are often gradual and less visible, miraculous works are always immediate and often far more public. In both cases, however, the gift of faith is essential. Faith precedes, accompanies and ensues the exercise of both the healing and the miraculous gifts. Faith, healings and miracles are related gifts of power.

Do Miracles Still Occur Today?

There are, broadly speaking, three views on this. There is first of all the liberal view. This is characterized by scepticism concerning the miraculous. Many liberals agree with Rudolf Bultmann, the famous twentieth-century German Bible scholar, that the very idea of miracles needs to be 'demythologized'. In other words, stories of miracles in the New Testament are myths not factual narratives. No one in an age of scientific materialism believes that miracles occur; therefore tales of the miraculous in the New Testament need to be treated as fictional not factual, as symbolic not literal. Then, secondly, there is the conservative view. The conservative looks at the Bible with reverential eyes and believes that the Word of God is inerrant. It contains no flaws and it never lies. Therefore, stories of miracles in the Bible are to be regarded as historical not as mythical. However, this does not mean that such events occur today. They may have occurred in the lives of Jesus and Paul, but they do not occur today. Indeed, miracles are understood to have ceased at the end of the first century (the philosophy known as 'cessationism').

Thirdly, there is the Pentecostal view (one also shared by the neo-Pentecostals or Charismatics) that miracles occurred in the Bible and they occur today. This view is known as 'continuationism' and stands in contrast to the scepticism of the liberal and the cessationism of the conservative. Pentecostals believe that miracles occurred in the New Testament and that they still happen today. In very general terms, the three views of miracles (which of course I am caricaturing) look like this:

LIBERAL: not then, not now
CONSERVATIVE: yes then, not now
PENTECOSTAL: yes then, yes now!

Which of these three views is correct? There is now a consensus that there is no evidence in the New Testament that miraculous works were restricted to the apostles or to the apostolic era. Paul makes it clear that the gift of miraculous works is given to members of the Body of Christ and that this gift like all the *charismata*, will be in operation 'until perfection comes' (1 Corinthians 13:8–10) – until Jesus Christ returns. Jesus promised his disciples that they would do 'even greater works' than he himself had performed (John 14:12). Like all the promises in the Farewell Discourses (John 14–17), this statement applies not only to the apostles but to all those whose lives are filled by the *paracletos*, the Spirit of Christ, in the post-Easter Church. Jesus therefore promises a continuation rather than a cessation of miracles. Indeed, his promise of 'even greater works' would suggest that there will be a larger number of miracles than Jesus himself had done. This makes perfect sense when you remember that Jesus' ability to perform such 'works' was restricted while he was incarnate as a human being. Once he had ascended to the heavenly realms, however, he could pour out his Spirit on all those who confessed his name. They in turn could perform *dunameis* (mighty works) through the *dunamis* (power) that he gave them. The miraculous works of Jesus can thus be done wherever Christians have faith for them!

The Pentecostal view seems to be true not only to Scripture but to church history. The fact of the matter is this: the evidence of history does not lend support to the idea that miracles never happen or that miracles ceased during the first century. In a recent article, Paul Thigpen has proved beyond all reasonable doubt that these views are not sustainable from the data provided by the history of the Church.[1] He shows that the miraculous gifts of the Spirit occurred beyond the first century and have been witnessed consistently up until and including our own. He quotes passages from Justin Martyr (*c.* 100–165) from 'The Shepherd of Hermas' (middle of the second century), Irenaeus (*c.* 130–200), Tertullian (*c.* 160–225), Eusebius (*c.* 260–340), Athanasius (*c.* 296–373), Hilary of Poitiers (*c.* 315–367), Martin of Tours (died 397), Epiphanius of Salamis (315–403), Augustine (fifth century), Severus (*c.* 465–538), Benedict (*c.* 480–550), Gregory the Great (*c.* 540–604), Gregory of Tours (*c.* 504–594), Aidan (died 651), Cuthbert (died 687), Joseph Hazzaya of Syria (born *c.* 710), Ulrich of Augsburg (*c.* 890–973), Anselm (1033–1109), William of Malmesbury (1080–1109), Hugh of Lincoln (1140–1200), Bernard of Clairvaux (1090–1153), Francis of Assisi (1182–1226), Catherine of Siena (1347–80), and many more during the Middle Ages, who clearly either witnessed, heard about or actually performed miracles. He writes of the decline of miracles during the Reformation, due to the cessationism of many of the Reformers, but he then speaks of the resurgence of the *charismata* in the lives of George Fox (1624–1691), John Wesley (1703–1791), Nikolaus von Zindendorf (1700–1760), Edward Irving (1792–1834), Charles Cullis (1833–1892), Maria Woodworth-Etter (1844–1924), Padre Pio of Pietrelcina (1887–1968), and many others in our own day. Not all of the evidence which Thigpen cites is of equal validity and credibility. Indeed, some of the texts which he uses contain the more 'legendary' material associated with 'hagiography' (writings concerning Christian saints), rather than the more factual material associated with reliable 'historiography' (history-writing). Nevertheless, Thigpen's doctoral research yields an impressive number of witnesses, and it is hard to disagree with his overall conclusion:

To sum up, we can turn to the words of Jaroslav Pelikan, a former professor of history and religious studies at Yale and one of the world's foremost church historians (not himself a charismatic): 'The history of the church has never been altogether without the sponta- neous gifts of the Holy Spirit' ... From the first century to the twenti- eth, from Antioch to Asuza Street, the accounts have been gathered and preserved to challenge the scepticism of unbelievers and to build the faith of believers. In the light of such overwhelming evidence, the Church today can look to the past with gratitude for what God has done, to the present with faith in his still-awesome power, and to the future with hope for the great miracles he will yet accomplish.[2]

Do miracles still occur today? The answer seems to be 'yes'.

Miraculous Works Today

At this point it might be helpful to turn to actual examples of the gift of miraculous works. In the following, we will be looking at the three kinds of miraculous works identified above: resurrection, nature and healing miracles. I am using the same source for these three examples, Mahesh Chavda's inspiring little book, *Only Love Can Make a Miracle*. The main reason for this is because I have seen Mahesh Chavda in action, and I am persuaded by both his life and his writings that he is a credible and trustworthy witness.

So, then, we begin with an example of a modern-day resurrection miracle. In his book, Mahesh describes a time when he was speaking at a rally in Kinshasa's Kasavubu Square. He had just finished speak- ing to the thirty thousand people gathered there, when he sensed the Holy Spirit saying,

There is a man here whose son died this morning. Invite him to come forward and receive prayer. I want to do something wonderful for him.[3]

Mahesh went back to the microphone and announced this, and almost immediately a man shouted, 'It is I! It is I!' The man's name was Mulamba Manikai. His six-year-old son, Katshinyi, had died of cerebral malaria that night; the medical staff at the Mikondo clinic had declared him dead at 4 a.m., after having tried numerous ways of reviving him (including holding a flame to Katshinyi's leg). Mulamba then left his dead son at the hospital and ran to Kasavubu Square, praying that God would do something wonderful. As he arrived, Mahesh stepped up to the microphone to share what the Holy Spirit had said to him. Mahesh prayed with Mulamba who then ran back to the hospital. When he arrived, he found his son had come back to life in his uncle's arms, much to the amazement of the hospital staff. Mulamba's family all believed in the Lord Jesus as a result of this miraculous work, and there was great rejoicing in the area. Katshinyi is alive and well today, and still carries the scar on his leg where the flame had been used in an attempt to revive him. The pictures overleaf show the English version of Katshinyi's notification of death on 12 June 1985.

Our second example is an incident best described as a nature miracle. Mahesh reports that in his work in Africa he has experienced many confrontations with sorcerers and witch doctors who have tried to disrupt his meetings. One particularly noteworthy instance occurred at the end of his campaign in the Kananga province. Having exorcized the chief sorcerer of the city of Mbujimai, Mahesh led the people in a prayer renouncing the evil in the area, and tearing down the stronghold of Satan in the region. The next morning news reached Mahesh of an astonishing incident which had taken place while they were praying. Apparently there was a tree outside Kananga (in Zaire) known as the Sorcerer's Tree. A number of sorcerers had been meeting while Mahesh was praying, and they had been calling down curses on Mahesh and the Christians in the area. Suddenly they saw fire streaking across the heavens, from the general area of the meeting. It shot across the night sky and fell upon the tree, burning it from the top. The leaves and the branches were consumed and only the trunk was left unscarred. Mahesh provides a photograph in his book, which clearly shows that this enormous tree (which had once stood over thirty feet high) had been consumed from the top down – showing that it could not have been burnt from the bottom upwards by a human hand. Mahesh concluded,

C.S.S.P.
C. A. D. Z.
Av. Kitoyi No 10 Q. Mikon'o.
Zone de KIMBANSEKE

Kinshasa 12./06./1985

N/Réf. :

V/Réf. :

Objet: Transfert - de Malade
KATshini - Malikai -

Cit. Médecin,

Je vous envoie l'enfant : KATshini - Sexe : Masc ♂
Age : 6 ans.

Pour a 4h.. du Matin au dispensaire avec
- Hyperthermie : T: 40°C T. A 7/5-
- conscill : Respiration : néant
Battement cardiaque - Coeur : néant
ne Réagit pas à l'injection
. Concl Δ - Paludisme
- déshydratation

N.B. DéCéDé †

Voir hôpital M. M. yemo pour un certificat
de décès.

Assist. Médical Resp.
IWANGA - EMBUM

Copy of the official Notification of Death from Mikondo Clinic verifying the
examination of Katshinyi Manikai's body on June 12, 1985. Listed are the
details of the examination and the concluding diagnosis: 'deceased'.

C.S.S.P.
C. A. D. Z.
Av. Kitoyi No 10 Q. Mikon 'o
Zone de KIMBANSEKE
———— — —

<u>Kinshasa</u> June 12, 1985

N/Réf. :

V/Réf. :

Objet : Transfer of Patient
Katshinyi Manikai

Dear Doctor,

I am sending to you this child, Katshinyi. - Sex: masculine.

Age: 6 years

Received at 4:00 O'clock in the morning with

- hyperthermia T 104"F B.P. 7/5

-Breathing : none

-Beating of heart: none

-no response to injection

-Malaria

-Dehydration

Note: DECEASED

See Mama Yemo hospital for death certificate

Medical Assistant in Charge
Iwanga Embum

The Notification of Death translated into English.

God is here. He is among us. He is with us in power and might. He is here by his Spirit to glorify his Son, Jesus, by doing the same works through his servants today that he did through Jesus – even to the raising of the dead.[4]

A third and final example concerns healing miracles. I will let Mahesh tell the story of his first meeting in Zaire:

> As I finished speaking, I heard the Holy Spirit tell me that there was a woman in the crowd who was dying of cancer, and to invite her to come forward. An elderly woman, her body covered with cancerous tumours, came walking down the aisle. As she neared the stage, the power of the Holy Spirit came upon her and knocked her to the ground as if by a physical blow. By the time I reached her, the tumours had disappeared. She rose to her feet and went away dancing for joy.[5]

Mahesh goes on to add that news of this miracle spread like wildfire, and that one hundred thousand people turned up for the evening meeting. Many crippled people were healed that night, including a number of little children. The manifestation of the power of God was so strong that many gave their lives to Jesus Christ, including sorcerers and witch doctors, who publicly confessed Christ as their Lord during the meeting. As Mahesh puts it,

> For them to take this radical step in public was a spiritual earthquake.[6]

So the gift of miraculous works is for today! Jesus Christ is the same yesterday, today and for ever. The miracles which he did in the yesterday of his ministry are being done by his faithful and fearless servants today. Where these miracles are clearly genuine, people are committing their lives to Jesus Christ. As in the age of the apostles, signs and wonders accompany and accredit the preaching of the Gospel, and many are saved on the basis of what they see as well as what they hear. No wonder then, that Pentecostals and Charismatics look at the Bible with such a different perspective. Having experienced the supernatural power of the Holy Spirit in their own lives, they do not relegate miracle stories to the realm of the mythical, nor do they regard them as irrelevant in today's Church. Rather, they approach such passages with what John McKay has called a 'doctrine of shared experience'.[7] In other words, they believe that their own experiences of the Spirit's power are in direct continuity with those of Jesus, the apostles and the earliest Church. The key which seems to unlock the door to such miraculous works in our own day seems to be three things: first of all faith; secondly, fasting; thirdly, compassion. Mahesh's book makes it very plain that it is only the person who believes like a child, who fasts with dedication, and whose heart is full of the wounded love of God, who will truly and effectively operate in the *charisma* of miraculous works. Only those who share in the fellowship of Christ's suffering will be used to minister the power of the resurrection to others. There is a cost involved, but the fruit is extraordinary.

Practising the Presents

There is a story in Acts 9 which tends to get neglected. The main reason is because Acts 9 tells the tale of Saul's encounter with the Risen Christ on the Damascus road and, not surprisingly, preachers tend to focus on that. But right at the end of the chapter, Luke tells the story of a resurrection miracle involving a woman by the name of Tabitha (Dorcas in the Greek). This passage provides some instructive insights into the actual practice of the gift of miraculous works:

In Joppa there was a disciple named Tabitha (which, when translated, is Dorcas), who was always doing good and helping the poor. About that time she became sick and died, and her body was washed and placed in an upstairs room. Lydda was near Joppa; so when the disciples heard that Peter was in Lydda, they sent two men to him and urged him, 'Please come at once!'

Peter went with them, and when he arrived he was taken upstairs to the room. All the widows stood around him, crying and showing him the robes and other clothing that Dorcas had made while she was still with them.

Peter sent them all out of the room; then he got down on his knees and prayed. Turning towards the dead woman he said, 'Tabitha, get up'.

She opened her eyes, and seeing Peter she sat up. He took her by the hand and helped her to her feet. Then he called the believers and the widows and presented her to them alive. This became known all over Joppa, and many people believed in the Lord. Peter stayed in Joppa for some time with a tanner named Simon.

A number of interesting points can be made about the practice of the *charisma* of miraculous works from this passage:

I. MIRACLES OCCUR IN THE CONTEXT OF GREAT NEED

It is a striking truth that there are many more reports of the gift of miraculous works in the poorer nations than there are in the so-called first-world countries. One of the simple and obvious reasons for this concerns the lack of good quality, free health care in those contexts. Another has to do with the greater sense of desperation; in the poorer nations, people tend generally to be much more desperate for God. In rich nations, on the other hand, there is a far greater sense of self-sufficiency. The relative wealth of people, combined with the widespread access to medical treatment, has made people far less dependent upon God for the bare necessities of life. In the story above, it is worthwhile remembering that Tabitha was obviously a woman who ministered to the poor. It is also likely that she herself was poor (Luke implies that she was a widow). Whatever her own socio-economic situation, her priority was to make robes and other clothing for the underprivileged in Joppa. When she died of an unspecified illness, many people were consequently deprived not only of a person who ministered in the *charismata* of mercy and helpful deeds, but also of a source of basic assistance. The context for this particular miracle is therefore one of great poverty. Like the story involving Mahesh and Katshinyi, the tale of Tabitha reveals God's bias to the poor and his desire to reach out to them with the power of his love. If we in the wealthier nations want to see the gift of miraculous works in greater measure, then we too must be prepared to go to places of great need and to learn to be more desperate for God.

2. MIRACLES OCCUR IN AN ATMOSPHERE OF FAITH

In the story of Tabitha, there is evidence of charismatic faith. There is, for example, the faith of Tabitha's friends. They refuse to put her body in a tomb, the normal burial custom. Instead, having heard that Peter is nearby, they wash it in accordance with Jewish purification laws, and then lay it in an upstairs room. The clear implication is that they have faith that God will use Peter to do a remarkable, supernatural work. For this reason, the disciples in Joppa send two men off to Lydda, a nearby town where Peter has been ministering. The message they send is for him to come at once. The reason they send it is because they fully anticipate a great miracle. This should remind us that God does great things for those who expect great things.

Cast your mind back to the story of Katshinyi again for a moment. Think of the faith of Katshinyi's father as he ran to the rally in order to ask Mahesh to come and pray for his son. Listen to what he thought as he ran:

I had no money, so I left my son's body at the hospital, with my brother. I went to the company where I worked, to see if I could borrow some money. As I stepped into the street, I prayed, 'You are the great God. If it gives you glory for Katshinyi to die, then let him die. But if not, then let him live again. I have told many people that you are the Good Shepherd. How will they believe me if my own son dies?'

I remembered the story in the Bible where the woman Dorcas dies. Peter, the servant of the Lord, has just arrived in her city. He prays for her and she comes back to life. The Lord spoke to me then. He said, 'Why are you weeping? My servant is in this city. Go to him'.

I went to Kasavubu Square, where I had heard Mahesh preach before. As I arrived, he stepped back from the microphone. I was sad because I thought he was done praying for people. Then he went back to the microphone. He said, 'The Lord has shown me that there is a man here whose son has died this morning. Come forward and the Lord will do something wonderful'.

I went running to the front. Mahesh prayed for me. I felt great joy. I felt faith inside me. I knew God would answer these prayers. I ran back to the hospital right away.[8]

Miraculous works occur when people, out of sheer desperation, take hold of God's Word and believe in it with the passionate simplicity of a child. For those of us who tend to be over-sophisticated in our dealings with God, this is a salutary reminder.

3. MIRACLES OCCUR THROUGH TRUE DISCIPLES

We need to remember that Peter was a learner. The word 'disciple' (*mathetes* in Greek) means a 'learner'. It refers primarily to one who learns from their Rabbi and Master. Peter was certainly a learner in this sense. We should note in particular the way in which Peter imitates the actions of Jesus in this story. In Luke 8:49–56 we read of another resurrection miracle, this time involving the twelve-year-old daughter of a man called Jairus. Jairus, a ruler of the local synagogue, falls at Jesus' feet and implores Jesus to help his only daughter, who is dying. Jesus goes to his house and takes Peter, James and John into the room where the girl lies dead. Jesus tells all the mourners to leave (with the exception of the girl's parents). He takes her by the hand and utters the words, '*Talitha, coum,*' which in Aramaic means 'Little girl, get up.' At once she stands up, much to the astonishment of her parents.

It is obvious that Peter was greatly impressed by Jesus' ministry to Jairus' daughter because some of his actions seem to be a kind of *imitatio Christi* ('imitation of Christ'). Like Jesus, Peter dismisses the mourners from the room. Like Jesus, Peter utters a word of command for the person to get up; indeed, in Aramaic (the original language of both Jesus and Peter) there are some remarkable similarities:

Jesus: '*Talitha, coum*' – 'Little girl, get up!'
Peter: '*Tabitha, coum*' – 'Tabitha, get up!'

Like Jesus, Peter takes hold of the girl's hand. Evidently then, Peter was a learner. Having been in that room when Jesus raised Jairus' daughter, he had learned how to operate 'the Jesus way', as it were. Those who want to operate in the gift of miraculous works should remember that this gift is given only to those who are disciples in the real sense of the word, i.e. 'those who learn from Jesus'. Mahesh Chavda is certainly one of those. As he puts it:

My vision is to fulfil Jesus' command to take the gospel to all the earth with signs and wonders following. When people see the miracles of God in their midst, they know the message of the Gospel is true. I want all men and women to be able to obey the words of Jesus: 'Go back and report what you have seen and heard: the blind receive sight, the lame walk, those who have leprosy are cured, the deaf hear, the dead are raised, and the good news is preached to the poor.'

(Luke 7:22)[9]

4. MIRACLES OCCUR WHEN COMPASSION PREVAILS

Mahesh Chavda's book about miracles is called, *Only Love Can Make a Miracle*. The emphasis throughout is on the importance of compassion in the context of miraculous works. Indeed, the book reveals that Mahesh only started to minister in the miraculous after a period working in a school for children with the most appalling mental, physical and social problems. He worked there because God called him to be an ambassador of divine love to those whom the world forgets. Towards the end of the book, Mahesh prays for a number of people who are desperately ill, including one woman who is covered with sores. She thanks him for having the love to touch her, and as tears flow from Mahesh's eyes, he hears the Lord say the following words:

The way you see these people is the way I see the nations. I feel compassion for them. They are hurting. They are hungry, like this woman, for anything they can receive from me. I want to send my Church to them, to touch them, to pray for them, to feed them, to heal them. But my Church is hiding as if in a cave, turning its face from the poor and the needy, hardening its heart against the nations.[10]

If miracles are to happen, then compassion must prevail.

In the case of Peter and Tabitha, there is a hint of the victory of compassion over prejudice. If we are to see how this happens, then it is important to read the story from a Jewish perspective. From a Jewish point of view, what the mourners ask of Peter requires great love on his part. Even though Tabitha's body has been carefully washed, it is still true to say that Peter has to overcome certain religious prejudices before he can minister in the gift of miraculous works. For a Jewish man like Peter it was no easy thing to enter the room where a corpse lay, yet love prevailed in this instance. The compassion of God welled up inside Peter's heart to such a degree that Peter forgot the prejudices of his religious upbringing. At the end of the story we see an even clearer sign of this, with Peter staying at the house of a tanner called Simon. Tanners traded in the skins of dead animals, and dead animals were regarded by Jews as impure – like dead humans! Peter, however, is learning that the love of God prevails over human prejudice, and this in turn is excellent preparation for his next adventure in Acts 10, which involves Peter having to overcome his prejudices concerning the Gentile Cornelius and his household (and that after a vision of profane meat!). So miracles occur when compassion prevails. As Mahesh says, 'the power of God is to be found in the love of God.'

5. MIRACLES OCCUR WHEN WE LOOK UP TO GOD

There is a very important detail in verse 40 of our story. Once Peter had entered the room where Tabitha lay, Luke says that Peter got down on his knees to pray. What Luke says next is very revealing:

> *Turning towards the dead woman*, he said, 'Tabitha, get up!' She opened her eyes, and seeing Peter, she sat up.

The key words here are, 'turning towards the dead woman'. What do they signify? They reveal that Peter, when he went alone into the room, did not look first at the corpse but at God. He got down on his knees and looked up to heaven. That was his first priority. Then, having spent time reminding himself of the greatness of God, he turned to the dead woman and addressed her with a simple, direct command. The abiding lesson to be learnt from this is the importance of beholding the glory of the Lord before tackling the deathly situations which surround us so much of the time. Only those who recognize that we have a great God, who acknowledge that we have a 'Big Jesus' and a 'tiny Satan', and who know in their hearts that nothing can stop the Holy Spirit – only men and women of *this* level of uncluttered faith can operate in the gift of miraculous works. Mahesh is one such person.

Miracles and the Future

C. S. Lewis once said that 'miracles are for beginners'. If that is really true, then I want to be a beginner for the rest of my life! The truth is that the gift of miraculous works is available to the Church of Jesus Christ today. The question is, are we going to have the faith to use it? Or are we going to ignore it out of intellectual pride? When Paul wrote his letter to the Galatians he asked,

> Does God give you his Spirit and work miracles among you because you observe the law, or because you believe what you heard?
>
> (Galatians 3:5)

These words demonstrate that the earliest Christians experienced miracles on a regular basis. When they believed the message of the Gospel, they received the Holy Spirit and God worked miracles among them. The words translated, 'God works miracles among you,' are in the present continuous tense in the Greek: 'God continually works miracles among you.' What further evidence could we have for the great gap between the contemporary Church and the churches of the New Testament? In the first-century Church, people experienced a constant supply of the Holy Spirit and frequent manifestations of God's miraculous power. They did so because they simply believed what they heard. Today, so much of the Church is characterized by scepticism rather than faith, and as a result there is far too little evidence of the miraculous. Of course, miracles do not always happen, even when people like Mahesh pray for them. Mahesh's book contains at least one example of that truth. But I would rather be a member of a church where people dared to ask for miracles than a member of one that never asked at all. I would rather be a member of a church characterized by simple faith than a member of a church characterized by sophisticated scepticism. As John Wimber has often pointed out, no one in the

New Testament ever got healed in response to the words, 'Your scepticism has made you well'. No one will today, either.

For me the great beauty of miracles lies in their relationship to the kingdom of God. The kingdom of God has been inaugurated in Jesus' first coming and will be consummated in his second. Miracles are signs of the kingdom; they are outward signs of the invisible, dynamic rule of God. When Christ returns on the last day, the promise of Scripture is that God will create new heavens and a new earth out of the fabric of the existing heavens and earth. He will perform the miracle of immediate, cosmic recreation. In the meantime, every person who witnesses a miracle in the name of Jesus is witnessing a 'trailer' of the eschatological re-creation of the world. Every time a dead person is raised to life, we catch a glimpse of the unimaginable miracle of the final resurrection of the dead at the *parousia*. Every time a person is miraculously healed, we are given a foretaste of the wholeness which will be ours as we feed from the leaves of the tree of life in heaven. Every time God intervenes in nature to multiply loaves or to calm storms, we are given a hint of 'Paradise Regained' – nature once again under the sovereign rule of God. The great beauty of the gift of miraculous works is that it affords us a momentary 'apocalypse' or 'unveiling' of tomorrow's world. As such, the nearer we get to God's Tomorrow, the more we can expect to see miracles occur. So, Lord, let the miracles happen in our midst! Let your kingdom come, and let there be signs and wonders throughout the world.

Questions

1 Have you ever witnessed or heard about a nature miracle, a resurrection miracle, or a healing miracle?
2 Do you expect miracles to happen today?
3 If so, do you expect them to happen as a result of your prayers?
4 What is the attitude towards miracles in your church?
5 Do you feel that there is an increase in the number of miracles today?
6 How do you distinguish between a genuine miracle and a counterfeit one?
7 What kind of scientific criteria would have to be satisfied for something to be classified as a miracle?[11]

8   Can the devil inspire counterfeit miracles?
9   If so, what might be his purpose?
10   What is the purpose of genuine miracles?

Prayer

Lord Jesus Christ, in your earthly ministry you healed the sick, you raised the dead and you calmed the storms. We believe you are the same yesterday, today and for ever. What you did yesterday, we ask that you would do through us today. What you do in us today, we pray would give us a glimpse of what you intend to do tomorrow. Give us more faith, O Lord. Grant us more of your compassion. Let the blind see, the lame walk, the deaf hear, the dead be raised, the demonized set free, and the poor given dignity and love. Raise your Church to life in the miracle-working power of your Spirit, that it may in turn bring life to a dying planet. These things we ask in your holy and majestic name. Amen.

SIX

The Gift of Prophecy

Of all the grace-gifts it is probably prophecy which has received most attention in recent years. The main reason for this lies in the simple fact that there has been a noticeable increase in the use of this gift in the churches today. I myself have been greatly blessed by those who have operated in this gift in an authentic and a humble way. Indeed, I would go so far as to say that I have been handed a number of prophetic words which have been of great value in terms of personal and corporate guidance. At the same time, however, I feel bound to confess that I have also suffered at the hands of those who have claimed to have this gift, but have used that claim as a means of manipulation and control. So my feelings are understandably mixed. On the one hand, where the gift is genuine, I regard it as a priceless blessing to the Church. On the other hand, where it is false, I see it as something which is potentially destructive and hurtful. Having had both positive and negative experiences, I therefore want to say at the outset that this chapter represents the outcome of a good deal of reflection at both a pastoral and an academic level. My prayer is that it will help others – particularly church leaders – as they seek to steward this anointing with the wisdom required. The position which I would like to encourage people to take in this area can be summed up by the following three guidelines:

mixed feelings

Welcome the gift of prophecy
Be **Wise** in how you handle prophets
Weigh every purported prophecy

The Nature of Prophecy

In his list of the grace-gifts in 1 Corinthians 12:8–10, Paul says 'to another [is given] prophecy (*propheteia*)'. What did Paul mean by *propheteia*? This is an important question because there are several misconceptions about prophecy in evangelical circles today. The first of these concerns 'foretelling'. Some charismatic evangelicals have made the mistake of defining the gift of prophecy solely in terms of predicting the future. Now there is little doubt that prophecy can have a predictive element. However, prophecy is much more about 'forthtelling' God's word in a particular situation, and not just about foretelling the future. That brings me to the second common misconception, which concerns the notion of 'forthtelling'. The idea that prophecy is 'forthtelling the Word of the Lord' has led many conservative evangelicals to conclude that prophecy is the same as preaching. Since preaching is a declaration of what God has said in his written Word, they argue that prophecy must be preaching. However, this again is a reductionist definition. While there is little doubt that anointed preaching can have a prophetic dimension to it, the New Testament does not allow us to confuse the gift of prophecy with preaching or teaching. Indeed, Paul himself makes a distinction between the gift of teaching and the gift of prophecy. It is therefore imperative to begin with a clear, concise definition of how Paul understood this gift, in contradistinction to what we would like him to have meant!

One of the best discussions of the gift of prophecy is in James Dunn's book, *Jesus and the Spirit*. There the author makes an important distinction between the gift of teaching and the gift of prophecy. He sees the charisma of teaching as an inspired insight into the Word of God. In other words, teaching is 'charismatic exegesis'. It is a fresh understanding of the significance of the written Word (which, in Paul's time, was primarily the Old Testament).

Prophecy, on the other hand, is an inspired utterance of a word which God gives directly to the believer. It is 'the speaking forth of words given by the Spirit in a particular situation'. Thus, neither teaching nor prophecy are natural aptitudes or talents. As grace-gifts they are to be regarded as the work of the Spirit in our lives. Both are charismatic endowments. However, their difference lies in this: while teaching has a conservative function, prophecy has a creative function. The gift of teaching involves a charismatic revelation concerning the Scriptures – a new insight into the written Word. The gift of prophecy involves a charismatic revelation which is consistent with the Scriptures – a fresh insight in accordance with the written Word. As Dunn puts it:

> For Paul prophecy is a word of revelation. It does not denote the delivery of a previously prepared sermon; it is not a word that can be summoned up to order, or a skill that can be learned; it is a spontaneous utterance, a revelation given in words to the prophet to be delivered as it is given.[1]

How, then, is such 'immediate' revelation imparted? Mark Cartledge has written a helpful article on the 'prophetic experience', as he calls it.[2] He argues that there are three possible ways of viewing the prophetic experience. The first category consists of a message being received some time before it is actually shared. In other words, a person receives revelation but waits minutes, hours or even days before sharing it. The second category consists of a part of a message being received by a person, and the rest being received as the person speaks out. Thus, a person starts to utter an incomplete message, and the message is completed as she or he speaks out in faith. The third and final category consists of an impulse to prophesy, but without any words in one's mind to share. In this scenario, the person feels a compulsion to stand and utter a word of prophecy, and that word comes in its entirety as she or he starts to speak. As far as the 'prophetic experience' is concerned, these three models do seem to me to cover the vast majority of cases which I myself have witnessed. They also provide a helpful framework for discussing the reception and the relay of prophetic words.

To summarize, then, the gift of prophecy consists of the following: 1. A spontaneous, Spirit-inspired compulsion to speak out a message of revelation. 2. A sense of words coming to mind. This can either be a complete message, a partial message, or just a sense that the message will come as you start speaking. 3. The actual utterance of this message, either immediately, or after a delay of minutes, hours, even days.

The Forms of Prophecy

Paul writes, 'if a revelation comes to someone who is sitting down, the first speaker should stop' (1 Corinthians 14:30). He is talking in this context of the use of the gift of prophecy. A number of things can be inferred from this passage. First of all, it is immediately clear that prophecy is 'revelation'. The word Paul uses is *apokalupthe*, a verb which indicates a sovereign act of divine disclosure. This further confirms Dunn's thesis that prophecy is a matter of inspired speech, not a prepared sermon. Secondly, there is a particular kind of divine action implied in Paul's statement, 'if something is revealed to one who is sitting'. That action consists of a sudden revelation of a word from God. It is as a person is sitting in the assembly that she or he receives, unprompted, an inspired message from God. Thirdly, the fact that the recipient of this revelation needs to stand up and utter this word highlights the fact that the gift of the Spirit is a gift of charismatic utterance. It is given to be given away to the Church, in the context of Christian worship. So 'prophecy' is a revelatory gift of the Spirit which is given spontaneously, in order to be shared with others verbally. As Wayne Grudem has defined it:

> Paul is simply referring to something that God may suddenly bring to mind, or something that God may impress on someone's consciousness in such a way that the person has a sense that it is from God.[3]

In what form, then, were such prophetic revelations given? Were they in the form of visions? Or dreams? Or messages? Or symbolic actions? Or impressions? Or feelings? Or even an audible voice? Paul does not go into detail at this point, so we need to tread carefully. However, one thing is clear: in Paul's thinking, the actual utterance of prophecy was something which was 'intelligible' to both believers and unbelievers alike. This not only tells us that the prophetic word was given in the native tongue of those present (unlike *glosso-lalia*), but also that the meaning of the words was not so elusive that people were left scratching their heads in confusion. Furthermore, Paul writes that such words, when addressed to 'unbelievers', were of a particular kind. They were a revelation of hidden facts about people present in the gathering. Thus, in 1 Corinthians 14:24–25, Paul states that an unbeliever (*apistos*) or an uninformed person (*idiotes*) who hears such words is convicted and judged by everyone in the meeting. Why? Because the secrets of his heart become manifest (*phanera*). From this we can conclude that at least one form of New Testament prophecy was an inspired declaration concerning the secret things (*krupta*) in a person's heart.

There are plenty of examples of this form of prophecy in both past and present church history. Often cited are examples from the preaching ministry of Charles Spurgeon. In his autobiography, Spurgeon records one amongst many incidents of this kind:

While preaching in the hall, on one occasion, I deliberately pointed to a man in the midst of the crowd, and said, 'There is a man sitting there, who is a shoemaker; he keeps his shop open on Sundays, it was open last Sabbath morning, he took ninepence, and there was fourpence profit out of it; his soul is sold to Satan for fourpence!'

Later, the same shoemaker gave his side of the story:

I went to the Music Hall, and took my seat in the middle of the place; Mr Spurgeon looked at me as if he knew me, and in his sermon he pointed to me, and told the congregation that I was a shoemaker, and that I kept my shop open on Sundays; and I did, sir. I should not have minded that; but he also said that I took ninepence the Sunday before, and that there was fourpence profit out of it. I did take ninepence that day, and fourpence was just the profit; but how he should know that, I could not tell. Then it struck me that it was God who had spoken to my soul through him, so I shut up my shop the next Sunday. At first, I was afraid to go again to hear him, lest he should tell the people more about me; but afterwards I went, and the Lord met with me and saved my soul.[4]

It is instructive to read how Spurgeon himself interpreted such incidents. He speaks of dozens of similar occasions on which he gave such words. He says he gave such words because he was 'moved by the Spirit', and also that he did not have the slightest knowledge of the people involved. When these words were accurate, he spoke of their effect on the listener as a 'smart hit'. More revealing still, Spurgeon compared this to the insight which Jesus had concerning the Samaritan woman in John 4, and says that the result upon his listeners was the same as that upon the woman of Samaria: 'Come, see a man that told me all the things that I ever did.' Today, the standard charismatic interpretation of this phenomenon would be that it was an example of 'the word of knowledge'. However, we have already seen that the 'word of knowledge' refers to something quite different. We have also seen that Paul refers to this kind of charismatic insight in relation to the gift of prophecy. Whatever Spurgeon's understanding of this phenomenon, one thing is therefore clear: prophecy is a revelation and a declaration of the secrets of an unbeliever's heart. Paul says in 1 Corinthians 12:24–25 that the result of this revelation is that the unbeliever is convicted and judged by all present. He makes the additional, interesting remark that the person will fall down on his face (*peson epi prosopon*). Thereafter, he will worship God and call out, 'Truly, God is among you!' (see Isaiah 45:14 and Zechariah 8:23). In other words, the sinner will be converted! As the shoemaker said of Spurgeon's ministry,

Under his preaching, by God's grace, I have become a new creature in Christ Jesus.

Is this kind of prophecy the *only* kind which Paul envisaged? The answer to that is 'no'. We need to note that the form of prophecy which we have just discussed relates to 'unbelievers'. Paul does not *explicitly* state that this kind of inspired disclosure of people's secrets was something which occurred in relation to believers. Paul is speaking about the response of 'unbelievers' to the exercise of the gift of prophecy in public worship. For them such words resulted in 'conviction' and 'judgement'. However, Paul also writes about the effects of prophecy on believers in the church assembly. In 1 Corinthians 14:3; he writes that

> The one who prophesies to men speaks edification and exhortation and comfort.

This indicates that the form of prophecy was not restricted to words which laid bare the secrets of people's hearts. Other words of revelation were heard as well. Indeed, we can surmise that any inspired message which had the effect of edifying, exhorting and comforting the Church could be subsumed under the umbrella of *propheteia*. That message could be expressed in 'indirect' as well as 'direct' modes of communication. In other words, it could come in the form of visions, dreams, pictures and even symbolic actions. As Peter puts it on the Day of Pentecost, quoting Joel 2:28ff.:

> And it shall be in the last days, God says, that I will pour out my Spirit on all flesh, and your sons and daughters will prophesy, and your young men will see visions (*oraseis*) and your old men will dream dreams (*enupniois*); and on my male slaves and female slaves I will pour out my Spirit in those days, and they will prophesy.

From Luke's perspective, the types of 'inspired speech' which could legitimately be described as 'prophecy' were quite extensive. The same was almost certainly true for Paul. We should therefore be careful not to restrict the form of prophecy to one form of address alone. New Testament prophecy was clearly more than the inspired revelation of an unbeliever's secrets. Indeed, Paul states that this is not the primary form of prophecy, because 'Prophecy is not for unbelievers but for believers' (1 Corinthians 14:22). The commonest form of prophecy was an inspired word which edified, encouraged and consoled believers. In the context of Christian worship, any inspired utterance which resulted in edification (*oikodome*,

[handwritten marginalia: edification]

[handwritten marginalia: prophecy is an inspired utterance that resulted in these things]

literally, 'building the house') could be regarded as a prophetic word. Any inspired utterance which resulted in exhortation (*para-klesis*, literally, 'encouragement') could be regarded as a prophetic word. Any inspired utterance which resulted in comfort (*para-mythia*, 'consolation') could be regarded as a prophetic word. The form of the address was therefore varied. As Rod Williams has said, 'There is no set form for the language of prophecy.'[5]

Thus, in contemporary charismatic spirituality, we find a number of different forms in which prophetic words are expressed. The most common form is usually a message of exhortation beginning with words like 'my children' and expressed as a word from God in the first person singular. Here is a good example:

> My children, I want you to look closely at the festal garment in which you would be clothed. I want you to see the dark thread which is inextricably woven into it, for it is the thread of suffering.
>
> It is the suffering of the Father, whose Son was slain before the foundation of the world.
>
> It is the suffering of the Son, who set his face steadfast to go to Jerusalem, enduring the cross for the joy that was set before him.
>
> It is the suffering of my Spirit who allows himself to be grieved by your wilfulness and disobedience.
>
> It is the suffering of my Church which is bruised and persecuted for my sake, yet not defeated.
>
> I want you to take my oil of joy for mourning, my beauty for ashes, my garment of praise for your spirit of heaviness. But you must realize that you cannot know the power of my Son's resurrection without the fellowship of his sufferings.
>
> If you attempt to remove the dark thread you will find your garment falling into holes, and you will be naked and a laughing stock before the eyes of those who have no love for you or for me.[6]

This is perhaps the most typical form of prophecy today: a word saturated in biblical allusions, usually in language which relies heavily on imagery (in other words, on 'pictures'). But there are other forms of prophecy which occur from time to time: visions, prophetic announcements about the nature of society, words about

God's purposes in history, dreams, symbolic actions, and so on. The variety of prophetic forms reflects the creativity of the Spirit.

The Authority of Prophecy

If God is speaking through the lips of people, then how much authority are we meant to ascribe to a prophetic utterance in the Church today? If a genuine prophecy is an inspired word from the Lord, does that mean that it has the same authority as the Bible, which is also the inspired Word of the Lord? Furthermore, if a prophetic utterance is inspired by the Spirit, does this mean that every word uttered by a prophet is authoritative? In asking these questions, we need to consider the writings of Wayne Grudem, a biblical scholar who has done a good deal of research into the authority of New Testament prophecy, and prophecy today.

In his latest work on this subject, Grudem begins by defining the gift of prophecy: 'telling something that God has spontaneously brought to mind.' He further clarifies this by saying,

> The words *prophet* and *prophecy* were used of ordinary Christians who spoke not with absolute divine authority, but simply to report something that God had laid on their hearts or brought to their minds.[7]

In this respect, Grudem rightly distinguishes the gift of prophecy from that of teaching:

> The distinction is quite clear: if a message is the result of conscious reflection on the text of Scripture, containing interpretation of the text and application to life, then it is (in New Testament terms) a teaching. But if a message is the report of something that God brings suddenly to mind, then it is a prophecy.[8]

For Grudem, then, a prophetic word is the utterance of something which God suddenly impresses on our consciousness, often in such a way that our train of thought is interrupted, always in such a way that we sense that it is of divine origin. Indeed, Grudem cites the following story as an example of what he means by prophecy:

> A missionary speaker paused in the middle of his message and said something like this: 'I didn't plan to say this, but it seems the Lord is indicating that someone in this church has just walked out on his wife and family. If that is so, let me tell you that God wants you to return to them, and learn to follow God's pattern for family life.' The missionary did not know it, but in the unlit balcony sat a man who had entered the church moments before for the first time in his life. The description fitted him exactly, and he made himself known, acknowledged his sin, and began to seek after God.[9]

fallible

Grudem's proposal is this: that even though such utterances are the result of what Paul called 'revelation', they are not to be treated as infallible. Indeed, the gift of prophecy is a fallible, congregational gift. It contains revelation which is partial rather than complete (1 Corinthians 13:9 – 'we prophesy in part'), and it is expressed in human rather than divine words. As such, Grudem insists that the authority of a prophetic utterance is linked to its general content and not to every word. Indeed, the very fact that prophecies have to be weighed carefully (1 Corinthians 14:29) shows that they are not infallible. As Grudem concludes:

> So prophecies in the Church today should be considered merely human words, not God's words, and not equal to God's words in authority.[10]

All this serves to underline the truth that contemporary prophecy cannot be regarded as equal to Scripture in authority. The main reasons for this are as follows:

1 Scripture is universal in application. A prophecy is merely contingent.
2 Scripture does not need to be tested. A prophecy does.
3 Scripture already possesses authority. The authority of a prophecy needs to be established.
4 Scripture is eternal. A prophecy is only temporary.

Prophetic words given today, when they are weighed and found to be genuine, must therefore not be invested with that absolute authority reserved for Scripture. However, they do have contingent authority in the situation concerned. If they are a genuine revelation of the mind of Christ, then it would be very unwise not to respond to them. In the example above, if the man had not responded to the missionary's word to return to his wife and family, that would have been disobedience. However, it would not have been disobedience against the one who gave the prophetic word, but against the Lord who inspired the word. It is not the one who uses the gift who has authority; it is the Giver of the gift, the Risen and Ascended Lord.

The Practice of Prophecy

All this inevitably leads us into a brief discussion concerning the way in which the gift of prophecy should be exercised in the Church today. From what has just been said, it is immediately apparent that every prophetic word should be uttered with humility, and not with false claims of absolute, divine authority. Grudem's advice at this point seems to me to be very sound:

> If someone really does think God is bringing something to mind which should be reported in the congregation, there is nothing wrong with saying, '*I think* the Lord is putting on my mind that ...' or '*It seems to me that* the Lord is showing us ...' or some similar expression. Of course that does not sound as 'forceful' as 'Thus says the Lord', but if the message is really from God, the Holy Spirit will cause it to speak with great power to the hearts of those who need to hear.[11]

So the first principle for the practice of prophecy is this: be humble in the way you offer a word of prophecy. Do not claim to be 100 per cent accurate in the prophetic revelation which you receive (as one self-styled prophet once claimed in my presence). Let us acknowledge the fallibility which is an inevitable consequence of our humanity, and be humble in the way we offer a word of prophecy.

The second principle is this: be loving in the way you offer the (2) word. Paul sandwiches his discussion of the grace-gifts of the Spirit around a beautiful eulogy of Christian love (1 Corinthians 13). The reason for this is simply because he wants to insist on a loving use of the gifts of the Spirit. Thus, in relation to prophecy, he writes,

If I have prophecy ... but have not love (*agape*), I am nothing.

If you have had the experience of receiving a word from someone who has not exhibited love, you will know just how hurtful an unloving use of the prophetic gift can be. If a prophetic word is being used to manipulate vulnerable people or to control leaders and pastors, then it is not a genuine prophecy, it is a false prophecy (Jeremiah 23:32). Paul tells us that we are 'to follow the way of love' (1 Corinthians 14:1). That is an imperative in the Greek. Those who utter a prophetic word should always do so in a selfless, loving way.

A third principle to be observed is this: be submissive in the way (3) you offer a word of prophecy. Remember that Paul, as the overseer of the congregation in Corinth, expected those who ministered in the gift of prophecy to recognize his God-given authority. He writes,

If anybody thinks that he is a prophet or a spiritual man, let him acknowledge that the things that I have written are a commandment from the Lord.   (1 Corinthians 14:37)

If we are to exercise the gift of prophecy in a biblical way, then we must remember that the prophet is subject to the pastor, not the pastor to the prophet. This does not mean that a person might not occasionally have a loving word of correction for a leader (as Nathan did for David). What it does mean, however, is this: that the one uttering a prophecy needs to do so in a submissive rather than an arrogant and domineering way. Furthermore, once a word of prophecy has been uttered, then the responsibility for weighing and using that word lies with the leaders of a church, not with the person who uttered the prophecy. This goes for prophecies which are orally delivered, and for those which are written down.

(4) A fourth principle is this: be self-controlled in the way you offer a word of prophecy. Paul makes this point in 1 Corinthians 14:32, where he says that 'the spirits of prophets are subject to prophets'. In other words, the prophet is in control of his mind, his body, and his spirit as he or she delivers the word. As Gordon Fee puts it:

> With these words Paul lifts Christian 'inspired speech' out of the category of 'ecstasy' as such and offers it as a radically different thing from the mania of the pagan cults. There is no seizure here, no loss of control; the speaker is neither frenzied nor a babbler. If tongues are not intelligible, they are none the less inspired utterance and completely under the control of the speaker. So too with prophecy.[12]

If a person utters a prophecy in an uncontrolled, ecstatic and extravagant way, that is not a sign that the word being uttered is from the Lord, nor is it a sign of the higher spirituality of the speaker. Far from it! Paul tells us that a prophecy should be offered in a self-controlled way. Those who exercise this gift must therefore utter the revelation which God has given them without theatrical show and without histrionic and hysterical behaviour. The spirits of the prophets are subject to the prophets themselves.

(5) A final principle is this: be faithful in the way you offer a word of prophecy. When Paul speaks of the gift of prophecy in his list of the *charismata* in Romans 12:6–8, he writes,

> If a person's gift is prophesying, let him use that gift in proportion to his faith.

If we are to exercise the gift of prophecy, we are certainly going to need faith. It takes faith to believe that the word on your heart is from the Lord. It takes faith to step out and declare that burden, even though you may not know the words you are going to say before you say them. It takes faith to believe that the word you utter will be weighed properly, and received without personal rejection. In short, it takes faith to prophesy! So, be faithful in the way you offer a word of prophecy. Recognize that you will sometimes make mistakes; however, making mistakes forms part of learning how to 'practise the presents of God'. If the church where you practise them is a place of love and acceptance, then you will have the freedom to fail, and the freedom to try again.

leader = conductor

The Administration of Prophecy

The leader of a church is rather like a conductor in an orchestra. His or her role is to recognize and use all the gifts of those in the orchestra, to train them to use their gifts in the best possible way, and then to harness all these gifts together to create a harmony which blesses all those who come to see and hear. In relation to Christian leadership, the analogy applies thus: the leader's job is to recognize the *charismata* which already exist in the community which he or she is called to serve. Thereafter, the leader's responsibility is to identify these gifts, and to train every member of the church to use them in the best possible way. In fulfilling this goal, the leader helps to create a fully-functioning, healthy and life-giving body. She or he creates holy order out of the charismatic chaos which exists in every local church. That holy order, in turn, is a harmony of love which truly commends the Gospel, and which the world truly wants to hear (John 13:35).

The role of the leader is therefore crucial in relation to the spiritual gifts in general, and to the gift of prophecy in particular. In this respect the leader has a difficult task. On the one hand, an over-controlling attitude towards prophecy will result in those with a prophetic gift feeling unloved and unwelcome. On the other hand, an overly uncritical attitude will result in those with a prophetic gift being inadequately trained, and the church becoming apathetic and even resistant towards prophecy. So just as there are some key principles for those who utter prophetic words, so there are some key principles for those called to oversee the use of prophecy in the church. Let me suggest the following:

1. Welcome the prophetic gift. It is clear that this gift was not meant just for the apostolic era. Paul certainly envisaged that this gift would be used until Jesus' return. We live in the inbetween times – between the first and the second coming of Christ – in which prophecy is still relevant. Therefore, as a church leader, welcome the gift of prophecy and welcome those who show signs of being able to use it.

2. Teach from the Scriptures about the gift of prophecy. It is so important that everyone hears from the pulpit that this gift is not some free-floating psychic phenomenon but a grace-gift which is described in Scripture. Public teaching from the Word of God helps to build confidence in the people of God. The key here is to combine realism with enthusiasm – realism about the dangers, the mistakes and the trivialities; enthusiasm for this gift when it is responsibly, wisely and genuinely exercised.

3. Encourage everyone eagerly to desire this gift. That is in direct obedience to Paul's imperative in 1 Corinthians 14:1. While Paul seems to have regarded only some in the Church as 'prophets' in an official sense (1 Corinthians 12:28), it is also fair to say that he wanted everyone in the Church to use the gift of prophecy. Paul therefore makes a distinction between the gift of prophecy and the ministry of prophecy. Not everyone has a ministry of prophecy, yet everyone can exercise the gift of prophecy. That is why Paul can say,

> For you are all (*panta*) able to prophesy in turn.
> (1 Corinthians 14:31)

Paul therefore believes that everyone is able to prophesy, but not everyone does! The prophet Joel had foreseen a time when God would pour out his Spirit on all flesh (Joel 2:28ff.). When that time came, sons and daughters would prophesy, young men would see visions, and old men dream dreams. Indeed, there would be a kind of 'prophethood of all believers' in which no one was excluded from the gift of prophecy. With the outpouring of the Spirit at Pentecost (Acts 2), that time has now come. It should therefore not surprise us to see Paul treating the gift of prophecy as an endowment available to all believers. As leaders and pastors, we should teach the same.

4. Carefully weigh every purported word of prophecy. Paul wrote that we are not to despise prophecy. In the same passage, he wrote that we are to 'test everything', and to 'hold on to the good things in a prophetic word' (1 Thessalonians 5:19-20). In 1 Corinthians 14:29 he encouraged prophets to 'discern' (*diakrinein*) or 'weigh carefully' what was said by other prophets. It is very important, therefore, that prophetic words are tested. If there is a constant stream of untested words in charismatic worship, then people's hearts will eventually become dull in the area of this gift. The pastors and leaders really must create the kind of environment where there is careful evaluation and honest feedback. In the next chapter, we will look at some of the criteria for evaluating prophecy in particular, and 'manifestations' of the Spirit in general.

5. Do not allow prophecy to dominate the worship. Paul said that only two or three prophets should speak at a time. Now there are basically two different interpretations of this command. The first is that Paul wanted only two or three prophets to prophesy during an act of worship. The second is that a leader could permit many prophecies in a meeting, provided that they were made in twos or threes and followed by careful evaluation. This second interpretation is the one favoured by Professor Gordon Fee. Speaking on Paul's words, 'Let two or three prophets speak', he writes:

> This does not mean that in any given gathering there must be a limit of only two or three prophecies. Even though that is commonly suggested, it lies quite beyond Paul's concern and makes little sense of v. 24 ('when you come together and *all* prophesy'), nor of the concern of v. 31 that *all* have opportunity to participate. Rather it means that there should not be more than three at a time before 'the others discern [what is said, is implied]'.[18]

My own view is that Fee's interpretation is correct. However, this does not mean that an act of worship should be turned into a stream of prophetic words, even if each one is weighed and tested in groups of twos and threes! Prophecy is just one of the grace-gifts of the Spirit (albeit a higher gift), and corporate worship involves more than prophecy alone (1 Corinthians 14:26). It should therefore be permitted to have its place, but not to dominate.

6. Encourage people into a listening mentality. Help everyone to recognize that prophetic words are received in an attitude of waiting upon God. They are imparted by the Lord when we cultivate the spiritual discipline of listening prayer. Prophecy is a grace-gift, yes, but it is most often given to those who spend much time in that secret place of intimacy with the Father. Indeed, intimacy leads to insight. Resting in God's presence leads to revelation (John 13:23–26). Pastors and leaders need to teach this truth not only by declaration (in the pulpit) but also by demonstration (in their own devotional life).

7. Maintain a sense of humour at all times. This is so important because many howlers are made in the area of the prophetic. For example, my friend Dave Parker (an expert on the prophetic gift, and indeed a genuine practitioner) often tells the story of a man who stood up in church and said,

> 'Thus says the Lord, "Just as Abraham led my people through the Red Sea, so I will lead you …" '

A few moments later, after an embarrassed silence, the speaker got up again and said,

> 'Thus says the Lord, "I made a mistake, it wasn't Abraham, it was Moses!" '

As leaders, we need to encourage a good healthy sense of humour when mistakes like this are made. That does not mean laughing at the one who gives the word. That is a bad idea because prophetic people tend to be extremely sensitive; they often need more pastoring than anyone. However, it does mean being able to laugh and learn together when words that are either banal or just plain silly are uttered!

8. Keep a sense of perspective. Nowhere do people get things out of perspective more often than in the realm of prophecy. Some churches fail to take prophecy seriously. Others take it far too seriously. In the first, prophecy is either neglected or disdained. In the second, people tend to develop a kind of credulity. For my part I like the attitude of Margery Kempe of Lynn. Margery was a fourteenth-century Christian contemplative who was highly 'charismatic' in the Pauline sense. She believed in the spiritual gifts and practised them too. She was particularly gifted in the whole area of the prophetic. Yet on the last page of *The Book of Margery Kempe* (subtitled, 'The Autobiography of the Wild Woman of God') she writes some very sensible words:

> Revelations are sometimes hard to understand. Things people think are revelations sometimes turn out to be tricks and illusions, and rather than giving credence to every intuition it's better to keep a level head and find out whether it's sent by God.[14]

That seems to me to be sound advice for our day as well. Margery acknowledged that she sometimes misheard God's voice. At other times she interpreted literally something which was meant to be understood spiritually. Margery therefore remained accountable to her church leaders at all times, and exhibited some good, God-given common sense where needed.

The Development of Prophecy

A final word is called for about the future development of the prophetic gift in Charismatic circles.

There are two areas which I believe require careful attention in the future. The first concerns personal sin. It is quite clear from our study of 1 Corinthians 14:24–25 that New Testament prophecy involved the exposure of hidden sin in people's lives. The prophetic gift was therefore far from safe. We all of us tend to exhibit the consequences of the Fall, the desire to hide. The rather disquieting thing about genuine prophecy is that it calls us out of hiding, and requires us to confront the secrets of our hearts. We must therefore be very careful not to indulge in escapism as we encourage this gift in the Church. So often we try to domesticate the Spirit by confining prophecy to words about hidden wounds and physical illnesses. God does want to reveal those things and, indeed, to minister to them. However, he is not just concerned about healing our hurts; he is also concerned about cleansing our sins. This means that from time to time prophecy will involve words of correction concerning our lack of holiness. As James Dunn has put it, 'there is a need in the assembly ... for a word of challenge and rebuke to careless or slipshod or detrimental activities.'[15] Provided that we can avoid the excesses of those who have abused this kind of prophecy, I believe that words which uncover sin can be of great blessing to our own spiritual health, and indeed to the spiritual health of the Church.

The second area where some attention is required refers to structural sin. If there is a problem with escapism in the use of prophecy (i.e. using the gift to address hurts but not sins), so there is a problem with individualism. Prophecy in Charismatic churches tends to be directed towards either individuals or the local church. There is very little today in the way of wide-angled prophecy – prophecy which addresses issues of social or structural sin in the world at large. Yet prophecy in the Old Testament, as Walter Brueggemann has observed, often involved a radical protest against the dominant ethos in society, and it also offered an alternative consciousness as well as an alternative vision for that society.[16] I have an impression that God may be calling Charismatics to cultivate the gift of prophecy in this way in the future. It would be good to hear prophetic voices lifted against the injustices of our day, both those which are hidden and those which are already exposed. Maybe it is time to break out of our individualism in the realm of the spiritual gifts, and particularly in the realm of prophecy.

So, as Paul put it, 'Follow the way of love and eagerly desire spiritual gifts, especially that you may prophesy.'

Questions

1 Have you ever had an experience of wanting to say something which God has laid upon your heart?

2 Have you ever shared what you would now understand as a 'prophetic' word with someone?

3 Is prophecy encouraged in your local church?

4 Are prophecies uttered in a humble, loving, submissive way?

5 Is prophecy handled responsibly and wisely by the leadership of your church?

6 Have you ever heard a prophetic word which resulted in the exposure of sin and the transformation of the sinner?

7 Have you ever heard or read a prophetic word which protested against oppression in the Church or in the world?

Prayer

Dear Lord Jesus, I pray for the Church in general, and for my local church in particular. Would you anoint both in the area of the prophetic. Would you please increase your anointing upon us so that we can all – including sons and daughters, old and young, rich and poor – operate in the gift of prophecy. Equip our leaders so that they may welcome prophecy and handle it wisely. Let prophecy come forth in all its varied forms. Let the prophets come forth, O Lord! And may you bring edification, exhortation and consolation to your people through the proper and right use of this gift. In your name. Amen.

SEVEN

Discernings of Spirits

In his list of the grace-gifts in 1 Corinthians 12:8–10, Paul writes, 'to another [is given] the discernings of spirits'. The word translated 'discernings' is, in Greek, *diakriseis*. This is a combination of two words, *dia*, meaning 'through', and *krisis*, meaning 'judgement'. The gift of discernment is, accordingly, the special ability to judge, evaluate and perceive something in the 'spiritual' realm. What, in particular, is this gift for? Paul says that this gift targets 'spirits'. Paul uses the word *pneuma* here, a noun used frequently in the New Testament, and with a variety of different denotations. The following table reveals the extensive use of this word in the New Testament:

	pneuma
Matthew	19
Mark	22
Luke	36
John	23
Acts	71
Romans	34
1 Corinthians	39
2 Corinthians	17
Galatians	18

Ephesians	14
Philippians	5
Colossians	2
1 Thessalonians	5
2 Thessalonians	3
1 Timothy	3
2 Timothy	3
Titus	3
Philemon	1
Hebrews	12
James	2
1 Peter	8
2 Peter	1
1 John	12
2 John	0
3 John	0
Jude	2
Revelation	24
Total =	379

There are three main ways in which the word *pneuma* is used in the New Testament. The first refers to the 'spirit' within human beings – to the psycho-spiritual part of our humanity. So Luke, speaking of Apollos in Acts 18:25, says that he was 'burning in spirit', i.e. a man of great spiritual fervour. When Paul says, 'Keep your spiritual fervour' (Romans 12:11), he literally writes, 'keep burning in spirit'. In these instances, the word *pneuma* could be translated with the adjective 'spiritual'. In other instances, however, the same word seems to denote a psychological attitude. Thus Paul, in 1 Corinthians 4:21, asks which the Corinthians would prefer, that he comes to them with a rod, or in love and a 'spirit of meekness'. Here a 'spirit of meekness' clearly denotes a mental and emotional disposition. This would indicate that *pneuma* can be used in both a psychological as well as a spiritual sense. Things are not as simple as that, however. The word 'meekness' (*prautetos*) is also used in connection with the fruit of the Spirit in Galatians 5:23 (*prautes*). If 'meekness' is a mark of the Spirit as well as a psychological disposition, then we should hesitate before making hard and fast divisions between what is psychological and what is spiritual. Accordingly, the word *pneuma* denotes the psycho-spiritual aspect of our humanity.

(2) The second main use of this word is in connection with the Spirit of God. When Paul says, 'God has revealed it to us by his Spirit' (1 Corinthians 2:10), the word translated 'Spirit' is *pneuma*. In 1 Corinthians 2:12 Paul speaks about 'the Spirit from God', and in 12:4, he writes that there are different grace-gifts, but the same 'Spirit' (*pneuma*). There are, in fact, many examples of the use of *pneuma* to refer to the Holy Spirit throughout the New Testament. Often the word is used to refer to the Spirit which is 'in Christ', or 'of Christ', or 'of God's Son', or 'of Jesus'. Often the same word is used to refer to the Spirit that is at work in the Church. It is often used to refer to the Spirit who inspired the Scriptures. It is also often used to refer to aspects of life in the Spirit (as opposed to *sarx*, the flesh). The challenge for the translator is to discover in each instance of the word *pneuma* whether it refers to the psycho-spiritual aspect of our humanity ('spirit' with a lower case) or to the Holy Spirit ('Spirit' with an upper case). The reason why this is a challenge is because the New Testament writers do not capitalize *pneuma* when it refers to the Holy Spirit. That is left for the translator to infer from the context.

So the first two uses of the word *pneuma* refer to the psycho-spiritual dimension of our lives ('spirit) and to the Spirit of God ('Spirit). (3) The third main usage refers to supernatural beings ('spirits'), these can be either benign or malignant. *Pneuma* is used for both angelic beings and for demons. It is used of angels in Hebrews 1:14:

> Are not all angels ministering spirits (*pneumata*), sent out for the service of those who will inherit salvation?

It is used of demons in Mark 1:23, 26, 27:

> And immediately there was in their synagogue a man with an unclean spirit (*pneuma*).

The unclean spirit (*pneuma*) shook the man violently.

'He even gives commands to unclean spirits (*pneuma*) and they obey him!'

To summarize: *pneuma* can refer to the human spirit, the Holy Spirit, to unholy spirits, and to angelic spirits. When Paul writes that there are 'discernings of spirits', he is referring to a particular kind of spiritual gift with a particular focus. He is talking about.

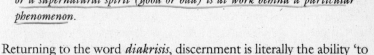

> the special ability to discern whether the human spirit, the Holy Spirit, or a supernatural spirit (good or bad) is at work behind a particular phenomenon.

Returning to the word *diakrisis*, discernment is literally the ability 'to see through' something to the motivating spirit or Spirit behind it.

Examples of Discernment

In the course of the Bible as a whole, there are a number of examples of the gift of discernment. Jesus exercised this gift to good effect on many occasions. He was particularly astute at being able to perceive and evaluate the psycho-spiritual nature of the people he encountered. A famous example of this is the occasion on which he met Nathaniel, and described him as ' a man in whom there is no deceit' (John 1:47). Jesus discerned that Nathaniel had a 'guileless spirit'. How did he do this? The gospel writer gives the answer in John 2:25, 'Jesus knew what was in a man'. He knew by revealed discernment what kind of 'spirit' a person possessed. The ability to discern the psycho-spiritual nature of a person is therefore very important. It is particularly important in the context of worship. As Rod Williams puts it:

> People who gather in the fellowship represent a wide spiritual range. Some may be present with a heavy spirit or an anxious spirit; there may be a weak spirit or a proud spirit; some may come with a jealous spirit

or a bitter spirit. Such spirits may not be apparent to others; indeed, the believers may not be fully aware of them among themselves. Yet such spiritual attitudes are likely to affect whatever happens in the dynamics of interrelationships. Hence, the gift of discernings of spirits can be of signal importance, for by a supernatural action – that of the Holy Spirit – the spirits of people are disclosed. When this occurs, the area of need may become apparent and proper ministry rendered.[1]

This statement should remind us that Paul is speaking about Christian worship when he describes the grace-gifts in 1 Corinthians 12. The gift of discernment, like all the gifts, is to be exercised when we gather together (1 Corinthians 14:26).

If the grace-gift of discernment can be used to perceive the 'spirit' of a person or a group of people, it can also be used to perceive whether or not the Holy Spirit is at work in a person. This is particularly true in relation to prophecy. In the list in 1 Corinthians 12: 8–10, there are at least two pairs of gifts. The most obvious is tongues and interpretation. Less obvious, but equally important, is the pairing of 'prophecy' and 'discernment'. Paul clearly saw the ability to distinguish between spirits as one which needed to be exercised in the context of prophetic utterances. In 1 Corinthians 14:29 he writes:

And let two or three prophets speak, and the others evaluate [those words].

The word which I have translated 'evaluate' is the Greek verb *diakrinein*, the verb form of the noun *diakrisis*, used in 1 Corinthians 12:9 for the gift of discernment. This indicates that Paul saw the *charisma* of discernment as one which is to be exercised in the context of prophecy. The New English Bible (NEB) translation of Paul's words in 1 Thessalonians 5:19 further bears this out:

Do not stifle inspiration, and do not despise prophetic utterances, but bring them all to the test, and then keep what is good in them and avoid the bad of whatever kind.

The 'discernings of spirits' is therefore an important gift. The noun 'discernings' is in the plural, and this could imply a regular, ongoing use of the gift in the Church's worship. In the context of Christian worship, the gift of discernment is particularly important for evaluating whether or not a person is speaking by the power of the Holy Spirit, or merely in the flesh alone. This process of discernment can sometimes be very simple, as when a woman gave me the following word in Norway recently:

> Our Father of Atom Energy wants you to go to Bangkok and minister to the prostitutes there. Before you go, you are to phone the Norwegian prime minister and chastise her for the religious prostitution in this nation.

It took only a few moments before I realized that this word was somewhat 'wacky' and certainly not of the Holy Spirit. On other occasions it may take a little longer to discern the source of a particular word. It also takes a certain measure of wisdom and courage to expose a word which is from 'the flesh' rather than the Spirit. The following example illustrates, in a humorous way, how discernment can sometimes take a few moments, and can sometimes require a bold step:

> Not long ago, a man went to the front of the church and said the following words, 'I have a picture. It is of a fish, a nail, a plate, and a hammer.' The man then sat down. There were a few minutes of silence before an elder of the church stepped forward. 'This is the interpretation of the picture,' he said. 'Stick the nail through the fish, smash the plate on the floor, and use the hammer to hit the silly man who just gave that word!'

If the Bible speaks of discerning the human and the Holy Spirit, it also speaks of the discernment of angelic and demonic beings. A good example of the former involves the prophet Elisha, who found himself surrounded in a city by the army of the King of Syria. Elisha told his servant not to be afraid because those who were with them far outnumbered those who were against them. Elisha was referring here to the angelic hosts. His servant could not initially see these angelic beings, so Elisha prayed that his servant would be given discernment to see them. The servant then saw that the mountain was full of horses and chariots of fire (2 Kings 6:16–17). So discernment can sometimes reveal the presence of angels. This is certainly true in the context of Christian worship. Here is Rod Williams again:

> It is quite possible that someone gifted with the discernings of spirits may perceive God's presence and that of his angels. So a contemporary chorus testifies:
>
> *Surely the presence of the Lord is in this place.*
> *I can feel His mighty power and His grace,*
> *I can hear the brush of angels' wings,*
> *I see glory on each face.*
> *Surely the presence of the Lord is in this place.*
>
> To hear 'the brush of angels' wings' (or however else the perception of angels may be understood) may well be the climactic experience in the discernings of spirits.[2]

To those who feel that this is an unbiblical thought, I need to say, 'Look at Hebrews 12:22, a verse about worship: "You have come to Mount Zion and to the city of the Living God, the heavenly Jerusalem, and to innumerable angels in festal gathering."' Evidently it is both a truth of Scripture and a fact of charismatic experience that angelic spirits can be discerned in times of public Christian worship.

The same, of course, goes for demonic spirits. Jesus often discerned a demonic spirit at work beneath the surface of a person's life. This same gift of discernment was evident in the early Church as well, as the incident involving Ananias amply demonstrates (Acts 6:1–5):

> Now a certain man, Ananias by name, together with his wife Sapphira, sold a piece of property. With his wife's full knowledge, he kept part of

the profit for himself and brought the rest to the apostles, placing it at their feet. But Peter said, 'Ananias, how is it that Satan has so filled your heart that you have tried to deceive the Holy Spirit, by keeping for yourself part of the profit from the land you've sold? Did it not belong to you before it was sold? And after it was sold, wasn't the money your responsibility? Why did you allow this course of action to be put into your heart? You have not lied to men but to God.' When Ananias heard these words, he fell down and died. And great fear came upon all those who heard about this.

In this instance, Peter exercises the gift of discernment of spirits. He perceives that Ananias (and later, his wife, Sapphira) have been motivated by a lying, deceiving spirit. Similar instances are recorded in Acts 13:6–12 (Peter with the magician, Elymas), and in Acts 16:16–18 (Paul and the psychic slave girl). Needless to say, in our own cultural climate today – where there has been an increase in occultism, paganism, satanism and mysticism – the importance of the gift of discerning evil spirits cannot be overestimated. We urgently need this gift if our worship is to exhibit manifestations of the Holy Spirit rather than any other spirit.

Criteria for Discernment

How is the gift of discernment exercised? What are the criteria for weighing up and seeing through *pneumatika* or 'spiritual things'? I would like to offer the following tests:

A) THE TEST OF CONVICTION

We need to remember that 'discernings of spirits' is not a natural ability but a gift of the Holy Spirit. Those who exercise it speak of a God-given awareness that something is either 'of the Lord' or 'not of the Lord'. When Paul was being pursued by the clairvoyant slave girl in Acts 16:16–18, Luke says that Paul eventually became 'greatly troubled'. This inner sense or intuition, which is an insight given by the Holy Spirit (as opposed to a 'sixth sense' or an innate faculty), is precisely what I mean by 'the test of conviction'. When, for example, a prophecy is inspired by the Spirit, there is a kind of 'resonance' in the hearts of those who have the gift of discernment. For them, it has a 'ring of truth' which leaves them with a sense of *shalom* or peace (1 Corinthians 14:33). When a word is primarily the product of the human spirit, there is likewise a sense of recognition that this word is 'of the flesh'. When a word is motivated by a demonic power, there is a plain sense of unease. Like Paul, those with discernment feel 'troubled'. All this may seem like an overly subjective way of approaching things. However, there is no doubt that even Jesus was 'troubled in spirit' when he confronted evil (John 11:33; 13:21). We cannot therefore ignore the intuitive, affective dimension of the gift of discernment.

B) THE TEST OF COMMUNITY

Paul obviously understood discernment as a gift with both a public as well as a private application. The most common use of this gift was in the context of charismatic worship. Thus, Paul insisted that all prophetic words which were uttered in worship should be weighed and evaluated. He also indicated that these words should be tested by a number of people, not just by the leader of the church (1 Corinthians 14:29). This means that discernment is a communal responsibility. When a word is given in public, there should therefore be time for the community of faith to respond with a 'Yes' , 'No' or a 'Let's give that one time'. The same goes for anything which is purported to be a 'manifestation of the Spirit'. The Bible teaches that the testimony of two witnesses is valid. Whenever something needs testing, we should therefore be looking for 'the inner witness of the Spirit' in the community as a whole.

C) THE TEST OF CONSISTENCY

Another criterion involves us asking whether a particular phenomenon is consistent with three things: a) the Spirit of Jesus; b) the Scriptures; c) the way God has clearly worked in the past. In relation to the first of these, nothing which masquerades as a pneumatic manifestation should be permitted in the Church if it is obviously inconsistent with the character of Jesus, as revealed in God's Word. Furthermore, nothing should be permitted which is evidently contrary to Scripture, however plausible or powerful it may feel. Likewise, if something has absolutely no legitimate precedent in church history it should be treated with caution. Though God is certainly able to do new things in both the Church and the world, it is likely in most cases that church history will offer us some helpful precedents when attempting to judge *pneumatika* or 'spiritual phenomena'.

D) THE TEST OF CHRISTOLOGY

Paul writes that it is only by the Holy Spirit that a person can truly confess that 'Jesus is Lord!' He makes this statement right at the outset of his discussion of the gifts of the Holy Spirit (1 Corinthians 12:3). There is more than a hint here of the inseparability of pneumatology and Christology. Pneumatology (the study of the Holy Spirit) cannot ultimately be divorced from Christology (the study of Christ). Why? Because the Holy Spirit always reveals Jesus (John 16:14–15), and he is the very Spirit of Christ. Therefore any spiritual experience which does not draw people's hearts towards the Lord Jesus Christ should be treated with suspicion. As the fourteenth-century Christian mystic Walter Hilton put it:

> Anything that weakens this desire for Jesus Christ and draws the soul away from concentrating on Jesus Christ is loosening the bonds between the soul and Jesus. Therefore this must come from the enemy and not from God. But if a spirit, a revelation, or a feeling makes a soul desire Jesus more strongly, quickly binding the soul to Jesus more firmly in love ... then you will know that this spirit is from God.[3]

When applying the test of Christology, we therefore need to ask whether a particular phenomenon reveals, glorifies, commends the Lord Jesus Christ and, in the process, succeeds in drawing us closer to him. A genuine manifestation of the Holy Spirit will be true to the orthodox theology of Christ. As the apostle John put it:

> This is how you recognize the Spirit of God: every spirit which confesses that Jesus Christ has come in the flesh is from God; every spirit which does not confess Jesus is not from God.

E) THE TEST OF CHARACTER

As we saw in the Introduction, Paul's instructions concerning the *charismata* are sandwiched around a call for sacrificial love (1 Corinthians 13). The reason for this lies in the social context of 1 Corinthians, which was characterized by a good deal of spiritual élitism and division – in other words, by the very opposite of love. Whenever a prophecy or any other phenomenon is being tested, we need to ask whether it was uttered or done in love. Did it demonstrate *agape* love? Did it promote *agape* love? As Paul wrote:

> If I speak in the tongues of men and of angels, but have not love, I have become a resounding gong or a clanging cymbal. If I have the gift of prophecy, and can understand all mysteries and all knowledge, and if I have a faith that can move mountains but have not love, I am nothing.

Where the *charismata* are truly in operation, the atmosphere will always be one of love rather than of judgementalism and élitism.

F) THE TEST OF CONSEQUENCE

Paul also speaks about the fruit of certain *charismata*. He is particularly precise about the fruit or consequences of genuine prophecy. True prophecy results in edification, exhortation and consolation. As Jesus said of prophets, 'By their fruit you will recognize them' (Matthew 7:20). This goes for all spiritual phenomena, not just prophecy. If they are truly motivated by the Holy Spirit, then we will see good fruit in the church in which they occur. If all manifestations of the Spirit are given 'for the common good', as Paul teaches, then whatever the manifestation is it will, if it is from the Holy Spirit, strengthen the community of faith. It will build up rather than tear down the church. The test of consequence is therefore an important criterion for discernment. However, we need to be realistic and recognize that this will sometimes mean a delay in making a judgement. It takes time to see what fruit comes from certain manifestations. We therefore need to be patient and diligent in monitoring the effects of any given prophecy or other phenomenon. For this reason alone, Paul's advice about limiting the number of prophecies in a meeting appears very pragmatic and wise.

These six criteria are therefore important in the whole task of charismatic discernment. Whenever we are attempting to weigh a spiritual phenomenon, we should always ask questions related to the criteria above. In brief, that probably means asking the following questions on the spot:

	Questions	Yes	No	Not Sure
1	Is your gut reaction that this is 'of the Lord'?			
2	Are others witnessing that this is the Holy Spirit?			
3	Is it consistent with the character of Jesus, as revealed in Scripture?			
4	Is it consistent with the Word of God and with orthodox Christian doctrine?			
5	Is this something which we've seen before and judged as authentic?			
6	Does it draw attention to the Lord Jesus or to someone or something else?			
7	Is it frenzied, uncontrolled and disorderly?			
8	Is it done/uttered in a loving manner?			
9	What kind of fruit do you envisage from it?			
10	Is this something 'for the common good'?			

Some of these questions may not be relevant for every spiritual experience. Others may require further reflection before a definite view can be formed. However, in terms of exercising the *charisma* of discernment, one should at the very least attempt to answer the first four questions straightaway.

Discernment at Work

Let us take an example. The following is not one which involves prophecy (the primary context for discernment) but a particular spiritual experience which, it has been suggested, is a 'manifestation of the Holy Spirit'. It is something which I have witnessed in a number of charismatic meetings since 1994. The experience in question is best described as,

> *a loud, spontaneous groan, originating in the pit of the stomach, uttered in public worship by one person or a group of people, who regard it as a burden for heartfelt intercession.*

This is currently a widespread phenomenon. However, there has been no serious evaluation of its source and significance thus far. Since we are encouraged to 'test' the spirits to see whether they are from God (1 John 4:1), we will weigh it here, using the six tests described above.

A. THE TEST OF CONVICTION

Here we enter the realm of the subjective. I have to say in all honesty that my own 'gut reaction' to this phenomenon has been mixed. On one occasion I have found myself near a person who was quite clearly faking this experience, probably as a means of gaining attention. On that occasion, and on one other, I have had that sense of inner unease which I associate with the discernment of something not of God. However, on the other occasions it has been quite different. I have been struck by the way in which whole groups of people (numbering over a thousand in some situations) have *spontaneously* uttered this kind of cry in response to a particular word from the pulpit. It is as if certain words – such as 'broken homes', 'aborted children', 'the lost' – act as a trigger, releasing a deep compassion which expresses itself in a loud cry for liberation. In situations like these, I have witnessed a chorus of sudden, non-verbal and passionate intercession which has moved me very profoundly. In those instances, I believe I have seen a genuine response to the presence of the Spirit – an outward, physical demonstration of a potent, inner work of grace.

B. THE TEST OF COMMUNITY

In worship events where the latter has been true, there has, I believe, been a shared sense in the gathering that this is a work of God, that it should be permitted as a spontaneous cry from the heart, and that it should not be stifled or quenched. When it has been genuine it has not been frenzied or abandoned. Indeed, there is a strange orderliness about it, with, as I have already said, whole groups suddenly crying out simultaneously and for the same thing. It has certainly been no more disruptive than the resounding chorus of 'Amens!' which often punctuates the preaching of Pentecostal pastors. It is certainly no more disorderly than the wonderful experience of corporate singing in the Spirit.

C. THE TEST OF CONSISTENCY

Is this consistent with the Spirit and the character of Jesus? At first sight you might think the answer to that would be 'no'. Surely Jesus never articulated such loud cries. If we think that, then we have not read the Scriptures carefully enough. We know that Jesus was in great 'agony' in Gethsemane as he prayed to God (*en agonia*, Luke 22:44). The writer to the Hebrews tells us that Jesus, in his earthly life, prayed in this passionate way, and that it was noisy:

> During the days of his human life, Jesus offered up prayers and petitions *with loud cries and tears*, to the one who could save him from death, and he was heard because of his devotion.

Here Jesus is described as offering prayers to God with *krauges* (literally, 'shouts') which were *ischuras* (literally, 'strong'), and with tears (*dakruon*, literally, 'sobbing'). These words reveal that praying with loud cries is not inconsistent with the character of Jesus.

What, then, of the Scriptures? Is the kind of experience I have been talking about here consistent with the Scriptures? Certainly there is a strong tradition of 'lamentation' in the Old Testament which could be mentioned here. More relevant still is Paul's teaching in Romans 8:26 about the work of the Holy Spirit in relation to intercessory prayer:

In the same way also the Spirit helps us in our weakness. For we do not know what to pray for as we should, but the Spirit itself intercedes on our behalf, with inarticulate groans.

Here there is ample evidence that the New Testament churches experienced a similar kind of charismatic phenomenon to the one experienced in Charismatic churches today. Paul describes it as Spirit-inspired intercession, which takes the form of 'inarticulate groans' (*stenagmois alaletois*). This is not, as some have argued, a reference to tongue-speaking because Paul describes tongues as 'languages' (*glossa*, 1 Corinthians 12:10), whereas this phenomenon is 'non-verbal' or 'wordless' (*alaletos*). Ernst Käsemann describes this phenomenon as 'ecstatic cries' and as 'visible manifestations of the Spirit'.[4] He relates it to the 'groaning' of the whole cosmos (mentioned in Romans 8:22) and defines this kind of charismatic intercession as 'the cry of eschatological freedom in which Christians represent the whole of afflicted creation'. As he puts it:

In this the Spirit manifests himself as the intercessor of the community before God and he takes it up into his intercession. By its ecstatic cries prayer is made for the whole of enslaved and oppressed creation.[5]

If this phenomenon is consistent with 'the Spirit of Jesus' and indeed with Scripture, what of church history? Is it consistent with charismatic phenomena which have been seen and welcomed before? The answer again is 'yes'. Larry McQueen has recently written about this phenomenon during the Asuza Street revival in 1906 and after, describing it as 'the prophetic pathos of Pentecostal lament'. He cites examples involving both private and corporate intercession:

I was seized with a spirit of prayer ... and the agony was severe, my bowels were much pained as I was drawn and bent almost double.

The first Sunday at the eleven o'clock service, at the close of the discourse a number of saints were slain under the power of intercessory prayer. This prayer, with agonizing cries and groans as the burden of souls was heavy upon them, lasted for several minutes. Not a few fell under the power of the Spirit and he prayed in them. This same power of intercessory prayer fell at several of the services.[6]

During the early days of Classical Pentecostalism, this experience of intercession was understood in terms of the Spirit 'praying through' a person. Indeed, 'praying through' became a common term for this intense communion with the Spirit of God. Clearly, the experience we are evaluating here is consistent with what God has done before.

D. THE TEST OF CHRISTOLOGY

Does this charismatic phenomenon of inarticulate, intercessory groaning pass the test of Christology? Does it draw people closer to Jesus Christ? In the case of the Pentecostal version of this 'lament', this phenomenon was seen as a communion with the prayer of the Ascended Christ. As one writer put it in the early 1900s:

> The heart [of Christ] is one living prayer, and he imparts to us the fellowship of his sufferings and prayer through the Holy Ghost. We do not always understand this prayer, 'He maketh intercession for us with groanings which cannot be uttered'. There is suffering. There is longing. There is conflict. There is deep agony. But God interprets and answers.[7]

In terms of Paul's charismatic theology of intercessory prayer (Romans 8), when the Spirit evokes this kind of prayer in us, we are joined to the passionate intercession of the Ascended Christ in heaven. As the following picture reveals, the Father gives us his Spirit as we pray. The Spirit then prays through us, joining us to the constant flow of prayer made by the exalted Christ and addressed to the Father (Romans 8:34):

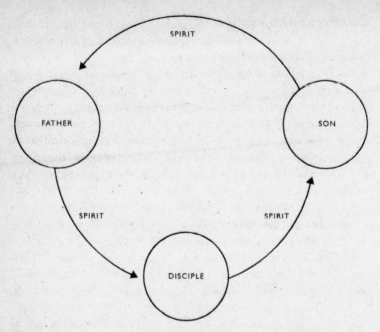

The phenomenon of inarticulate groaning is therefore not just a pneumatological experience, it is a Christological experience as well.

E. THE TEST OF CHARACTER

Is this a phenomenon which exhibits self-sacrificial love? The answer, again, is 'yes'. Intercessory prayer for the suffering world is one of the highest expressions of love. The kind of passionate, often tearful prayer which we are evaluating here is a demonstration of *agape* love. Here the believer groans with the whole of creation, crying out for that freedom which will come at the *parousia*, at the return of Christ. This, then, is the prayer of Calvary love. It is fellowship in the sufferings of Christ and, more specifically, the suffering of the Spirit of Christ in creation. As one Pentecostal writer put it:

> Shall not ... the pent up streams of Calvary ... flow forth from the broken depths of our own innermost being, convulsed and rent by the dynamite of the Holy Ghost?[8]

F. THE TEST OF CONSEQUENCE

Only a brief word is needed here. The abiding fruit of this spiritual experience has, for the vast majority of people, resulted in a renewed commitment to the discipline of prophetic intercession. Those who have learnt to cry out on behalf of the suffering cosmos have, in other words, been led into a deeper communion with the Lord in prayer. That is truly a sign of the Holy Spirit at work. Indeed, many have pointed to the significance of the sound made by people who are anointed with this gift of intercession: the sound of someone in labour. This again links in with the yearning for eschatological freedom of which Paul speaks in Romans 8. Accordingly, the best term for this phenomenon is 'travailing prayer'. It is the Spirit praying through us, crying out for freedom in the new order which Christ will one day bring.

The Value of Discernment

In my newspaper today I read an interesting piece about the use of 'noses'! Apparently Eurocrats in Brussels are funding a group of 'sniffers' to measure the smell given off by British workers. This group consists of fifteen researchers who have specially trained noses, and their job is to quantify the 'olf' (i.e. smell) given off by British workers. This panel of 'sniffers' has already been assessing 'olf ratings' in various offices and factories in Britain. As one of the team said,

> We go into an office building and the panel gives it a vote. We work out the olf load and from that we can calculate how much ventilation is required.

The main reason for the existence of this team is the fact that many offices contain materials which emit small amounts of invisible gas which can make workers feel sick. The task of these 'sniffers' is to identify sources of indoor air pollution and deal with them.

Perhaps you are already anticipating where I am leading with this rather incredible piece of news. Paul says in 1 Corinthians 12 that

the Church is the Body of Christ, and that each gifted person is like
a part of that body. If prophecy represents the ears of that body, we
might say that discernment represents the 'nose'. Those with the
gift of 'discernings of spirits' are like charismatic 'sniffers'! They are
endowed by the Spirit with the special ability to detect the *pneuma*
behind different phenomena. With that in mind, it is obvious that
every church needs a keen sense of smell. There is, at the moment,
evidence of an increase in the use of the gift of prophecy. There are
also signs of a dramatic upsurge in unusual spiritual phenomena. If
we are to judge such things responsibly, then the gift of discernment is essential. It is essential in the context of prophecy, where it
finds its primary relevance. It is essential in the realm of *pneumatika* or 'spiritual phenomena' in general.

Paul says 'to another [is given] discernings of spirits'. The plural
'discernings' indicates not only the frequency but also the flexibility
of this gift. It is a gift which is to be exercised often, and it is a gift
which is to be used in a whole variety of contexts – ecumenical
debates, ethical decisions, inter-faith dialogue, healing prayer, and,
above all, charismatic worship. As Francis Martin has put it:

> The age of enlightenment with its 'closed system' of thinking tend-
> ed even in religious circles to reduce discernment to prudence or
> character evaluation. With the abundant reappearance of spiritual
> manifestations, the true role of discernment has become once again
> apparent. Because the Spirit of God moves in the human heart,
> bestowing his gifts, especially that of prophecy, and because these
> gifts can be counterfeited by Satan and by the human spirit, we see
> the need once again to pray for the gift of the discernment of spirits
> so that we may know 'those things given to us by God'.[9]

This is a gift which we therefore need to desire. It is not a fashion-
able gift, like prophecy or healing. But it is necessary and a vital
gift. Like all the gifts of the Spirit, it must be used in a loving way –
that is, judging phenomena, not judging people. It must also be
recognized for what it is – a gift which involves both an intuitive
component ('gut feelings') and a rational component (theological
reflection). Handled wisely and well, this particular ability could

well prove to be one of the most priceless gifts in the years that lie ahead. May the Lord grant us more discerning people in his Church.

Questions

1 Have you ever discerned something 'by the Holy Spirit'?
2 Have you ever discerned the presence of angels in an act of Christian worship?
3 Have you ever discerned the presence of something demonic?
4 Have you ever discerned that a prophetic utterance was 'of the flesh' rather than 'of the Spirit'?
5 Is there a particular 'spiritual phenomenon' in your church which you might weigh and evaluate against the list of questions provided above?
6 What conclusions have you come to concerning its source and significance?
7 How has this chapter changed your view of 'the gift of discernment'?
8 Are there any in your church who have this gift?

Prayer

Dear Lord Jesus, I thank you for the precious gift of discernment. I ask that you would give me discernment in those areas of my life where I need special insight right now. I ask that you would give this gift to the Church, so that it may properly weigh the prophetic words and other spiritual phenomena which we witness. Lord, protect us from the extreme of credulity – of being gullible and accepting everything. Protect us also from the extreme of cynicism – of being dismissive of everything! Give us the right balance, dear Lord, for the good of the Church and the honour of your name. Amen.

EIGHT

Kinds of Tongues

We come now to the charismatic gift which became the focus of so much controversy in Corinth – the gift of tongues. Paul writes in 1 Corinthians 12:10, 'to another [is given] different kinds of tongues'. What did Paul mean by this? The first thing to say is that he meant something 'supernatural'. Like all the gifts, speaking in tongues is a charismatic endowment. Tongue-speaking, accordingly, is inspired speech. Some popular authors go so far as to describe it as 'miraculous speech'. Here is Timothy Pain:

> The spiritual gift of tongues is a miracle. It occurs when a human being prays to God in a language he has never learnt, and that must be a miracle.[1]

If the first thing to note is that tongue-speaking is 'inspired', the second is that it involves 'language'. Paul uses the word *glossa*, which is translated 'tongues'. Actually, *glossa* means 'language', not just the vocal organ known as the 'tongue'. Accordingly, the gift of tongues is a gift through which the Spirit enables us to speak unlearnt *languages*. Poythress calls this particular kind of language 'free vocalization', and he defines that as

> the production of connected sequences of speech sounds, not identified by the speaker as a language known to him, lexically opaque to

him, not capable of being repeated by him (except in very small snatches), and which sounds to an average hearer like an unknown language.[2]

The third thing to say about the gift of tongues is that the languages spoken by those who have this gift are diverse. In other words, different people speak different kinds of languages under the anointing of the Holy Spirit. Paul writes that 'to another [is given] *different kinds* of tongues'. The word translated different kinds is *gene,* and this indicates that there is a diversity of Spirit-inspired languages available to the speaker. You listen to a person speaking in tongues in one church, and he or she will sometimes sound different from a person using the same gift in another. That is not to say that every believer speaks an utterly unique 'tongue' or 'language'; indeed, recent research has revealed the remarkable similarities between tongues in one context, and tongues in quite another (even in a different continent, no less). But it does mean that the Spirit inspires a variety of languages. Thus, we can define the gift of speaking in different kinds of tongues as

> *a charismatic anointing in which a person speaks an unlearnt and unintelligible language.*

When Paul spoke about the gift of 'tongues', he was therefore referring to a complex phenomenon which in many ways resists our attempts to classify it. He was talking about a transcendent form of communication.

Different Kinds of Tongues

Tongue-speaking is not a monochrome phenomenon. It is a charismatic endowment which involves more than one kind of language. On the Day of Pentecost, Luke reports the following:

When the day of Pentecost came, they were all together in one place. And suddenly, there came from heaven a sound like a gust of violent wind and it filled the whole house where they were sitting. And they saw what appeared to them like tongues of fire, which separated and then came to rest on each one of them. All of them were filled with [the] Holy Spirit and began to speak in other tongues, as the Spirit gave them utterance.

Luke describes this particular type of speech as 'speaking (*lalein*) in other languages' (*heterais glossais*). In this instance, he is referring to the supernatural ability to speak in unlearnt foreign languages. This is confirmed by the fact that the many Jewish pilgrims nearby – who had come to celebrate the Feast of Pentecost from all over the world – heard the 120 disciples declaring the wonders of God in their own native tongue. This was not because they, as unbelievers, were experiencing a miracle of hearing, i.e. the supernatural ability to translate whatever the disciples were saying into their own language. Far from it! The Holy Spirit filled the disciples not the unbelievers, and, true to form in Luke-Acts, the consequence of that 'in-filling' was inspired speech. This leads us to the following conclusion: there is a type of tongue-speaking which can be termed *xenolalia*. This is

the supernatural, spontaneous ability to speak in unlearnt human languages, in such a way that the wonders of God are heard and understood by those for whom these languages are the native dialect (ta idia dialecta).

(Acts 2:8)

Is this the kind of language which Paul is referring to when he writes in 1 Corinthians 12 about 'the gift of speaking in different kinds of tongues'? There are a number of clues which suggest that he is describing something different. First of all, Paul is describing a kind of tongues-speech which requires 'translation'. There is much in 1 Corinthians 14 about the need for someone else to interpret or translate tongues when they are uttered publicly. When a person speaks in tongues, no one else understands him unless there is an interpretation (1 Corinthians 14:2). In Acts 2, however, the tongues are not 'interpreted' by a third party. They are straight-away understood by those standing nearby. Secondly, Paul says of the gift of tongues that it is something which is not understood by unbelievers (1 Corinthians 14:23). In Acts 2, however, literally thousands of unbelievers understand the 'tongues' which are being spoken by the 120 disciples, even though there is no public interpretation or translation.

When Paul writes about the gift of tongues in 1 Corinthians 12–14, it is therefore unlikely that he is referring primarily to *xenolalia*. I am one of many people who believe that Paul distinguished between two different types of tongue-speaking: *xenolalia* (speaking in an unlearnt foreign tongue) and *angelolalia* (speaking in an angelic tongue). What is the evidence for this differentiation between *xenolalia* and *angelolalia*? 1 Corinthians 13 – the great chapter on 'Love' – begins with words which are so familiar that we are likely to ignore their precise meaning and their true significance. Paul declares, 'If I speak in the tongues of men and of angels, but have not love, I have become a resounding gong or a clanging cymbal.' The part of this statement which is relevant here is Paul's differentiation between 'the tongues of men' and 'the tongues of angels'. Tongues of men (*glossais ton anthropon*) is seen by many as a reference to the phenomenon described in Acts 2:1–13; that is, the charismatic ability to speak in unlearnt foreign languages (*xenolalia*). Tongues of angels (*[glossais] ton angelon*) is seen by many as a reference to the phenomenon described in 1 Corinthians 12–14; that is, the charismatic ability to express one's devotion to God in the language of the angels (*angelolalia*).

In support of this differentiation, Russell Spittler has pointed out that *angelolalia* was not an unknown concept in the Judaism of Paul's day.[3] The *Testament of Job* furnishes us with an example of this kind of speech from a time roughly contemporaneous with Paul. *Testament of Job*[4] 48–50 describes Job approaching his death. As he prepares to die, he distributes his possessions among his children, reserving the best of his goods (a triple-stranded sash) for his three daughters. As the three girls try on each strand, their hearts are transformed so profoundly that they become indifferent to material concerns. The first daughter speaks 'ecstatically in the angelic dialect'. The second speaks in 'the dialect of the archons' (the heavenly, ruling powers). The third speaks 'in the dialect of those on high' (i.e. the cherubim). This shows that the concept of *angelolalia* was not unknown in the ancient world. It also gives us further grounds for suggesting that it is this phenomenon which Paul may be describing in 1 Corinthians 12–14 when he writes about 'tongues'.

There are therefore two main kinds of *glossolalia* (tongue-speaking) in the New Testament. There is the *xenolalia* of Acts 2 – unlearnt foreign languages which are spoken under the inspiration of the Holy Spirit – and *angelolalia*, the unlearnt language of angels, again uttered under the powerful anointing of God. While the first is addressed to fellow human beings (as in Acts 2), the second is addressed to God. The first is an example of inspired witness (hence its evangelistic value in Acts 2). The second is an example of inspired worship (hence its inappropriateness in the context of worship, 1 Corinthians 14:23). Paul was certainly aware of *xenolalia*, and he calls that 'tongues of men' (1 Corinthians 13:1). But his main interest in 1 Corinthians 12–14 is with *angelolalia*, the supernatural ability to speak in an angelic dialect. This does not mean that believers will never be given the ability to speak in unlearnt foreign languages. But it does mean that the most common form of tongues-speech is heavenly rather than earthly language. Thus, the gift of tongues is most often,

The spontaneous utterance of seemingly random speech sounds which represent the language of the angels.

The Language of Devotion

At this point it should become clear that we are dealing with a gift which is far from simple and far from uniform. It is, in fact, a complex and quite awesome phenomenon. As Timothy Pain puts it:

The thought of speaking in the language of Michael and Gabriel is not to be taken lightly: picture the exciting possibility of joining with the cherubim and seraphim, of participating on earth in their heavenly worship.[5]

Speaking in tongues is, more than anything else, a gift of adoration. It is an act of charismatic communication which results from an overflow of joyful praise from the very core of our beings (John 7:37–39). Indeed, we might call it 'the *jubilate* of the enraptured soul'. Thus, speaking in tongues is primarily a form of prayer. As Paul puts it in 1 Corinthians 14:2:

> Anybody with the gift of tongues speaks to God, but not to other people. Indeed, no one understands him; he utters mysteries with his spirit.

up!

This understanding of 'tongues-speech' as a form of prayer leads us to the differences between the gift of tongues and the gift of prophecy. The main differences centre on their direction and their purpose. The direction of tongues is upwards. The one who speaks in a tongue speaks to God not to human beings (1 Corinthians 14:2). The direction is always 'up'. 'Up' from the subconscious depths comes the impulse to praise and adore the Living God. That impulse is motivated by the Holy Spirit, and it causes the speech-motor centre of the believer to declare or to sing words which are unintelligible to the conscious mind. These words are words of praise which go 'up', as it were, to the heavenly realms. We can therefore portray tongues as follows:

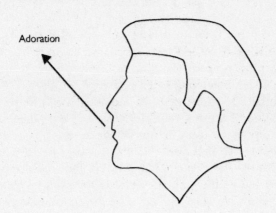

Adoration

In the case of prophecy, however, the direction of the mode of address is more horizontal than vertical. A prophetic word is given by the Holy Spirit and addressed to the Body of Christ. We can portray this as follows.

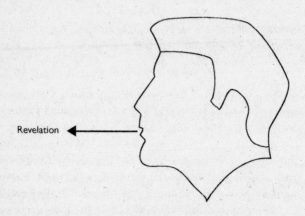

Revelation ←

For this reason Paul differentiates between the purposes of these two gifts. Tongues edifies the believer because it is primarily a private expression of ebullient celebration. Through it, the believer edifies himself as he shares in the secrets or 'mysteries' known to the angels. Prophecy, on the other hand, is an inspired utterance which edifies the Church. It is a revelation of the mind of Christ which edifies, exhorts and consoles the whole Body.

The conclusion which we must inevitably draw from this differentiation is this: that a translation of a public expression of tongues should usually be an utterance of adoration. Put another way, the interpretation of a 'tongue' is most often an expression of heartfelt praise. It should not really be a prophetic message of edification. In actual experience, of course, this is not always so. In Charismatic and Pentecostal churches, a tongue is very often followed by a word of exhortation to the church. Take the following as an example. This was offered as an interpretation of a tongue given in a meeting which I was actually leading:

You are a tall tree planted in good earth.
You will grow strong because your roots are feeding on me.
You will grow, and your branches will spread far and wide,
    reaching the whole world.
And your blossom will brighten all people,
    bringing joy wherever it is seen.
And your seeds will be many and they will fall
    and bear much fruit.
For you are my creation and I will give you water
    and you will grow in me.

In real terms, this is what Paul would have called a prophecy, not
the interpretation of a tongue. A wise and responsible pastor would
therefore have said something like this:

> That was a word of encouragement to the church, and like all words of
> encouragement or prophecies, we need to weigh and test it. However,
> what we heard before that was the gift of tongues. The interpretation
> of that will be a declaration of praise and adoration. Does anyone have
> the gist of what our sister has just uttered in the Spirit?

I have to own up and say that I did not utter these words in that
particular situation. I was subsequently corrected for that, and have
learnt – as we all must in the realm of the gifts – from my mistake!

The Limitation of Tongues

You might be forgiven for thinking from what we have said so far
that Paul would have had nothing but praise for the gift of tongues.
In fact, Paul is very ambivalent about it. On the one hand he can
say, quite understandably. 'I wish that every one of you spoke in
tongues' (1 Corinthians 14:5). It is, after all, one of the greatest
blessings to our private and public worship of God. On the other
hand, Paul can also express his reservations about this gift. There
are a number of reasons for this which we must now identify.

1. It is clear from 1 Corinthians 12–14 that there were some believers in Corinth who regarded tongues as the sign of a truly charismatic Christian. Those who spoke in tongues were the spiritual élite. Those who did not were second-class Christians. To correct this view, Paul puts this particular gift last in his lists, not first. Thus, in 12:8–10, he presents the *charismata* in this order:

> word of wisdom
> word of knowledge
> faith
> gifts of healing
> miraculous works
> prophecy
> discernment
> tongues
> interpretation

Later in the same chapter (12:28), he does the same again. He writes that God has appointed 'first of all apostles, second prophets, third teachers, then workers of miracles, then those who can heal others, then helpers, then those who administer the church, then those who speak in different kinds of tongues.' Paul's 'charismatic ecclesiology' will therefore not permit anyone to evaluate the gift of tongues above the rest. In the second list just cited, Paul even puts it after one of the most 'ordinary' and practical gifts – 'helping'.

2. Paul exhibits sobriety over the gift of tongues not only because of its potential for abuse but also because of its potential for ridicule in a public context. If a person speaks in tongues in public, an unbeliever will think that that person is 'out of their mind' (1 Corinthians 14:23). This reveals yet another limitation concerning the gift of tongues. 'Unbelievers' who hear tongues in public will think that the church is full of 'maniacs' (14:23, *mainesthe*). Paul goes on to say that the main reason for that is not because the gift itself is something evil or wrong, but because the unbeliever's heart is so hardened that even a demonstration of a 'sign' as supernatural as *glossolalia* will not convince him that God is truly present

(1 Corinthians 14:20–25). Only prophecy will do that, because prophetic utterances reveal the sinful secrets of the unbeliever's heart, and result in a sense of conviction not only of his sinfulness but also of God's reality. The public use of the gift of tongues, on the other hand, has the potential for ridicule and disdain from unbelievers.

3. Paul is also realistic about another limitation. He writes that the public use of tongues is really quite redundant without an accompanying interpretation. He points to the folly of entering an assembly and speaking in tongues without an attendant, intelligible utterance (1 Corinthians 14:6). That would be like making a tuneless noise on a harp, or an unclear sound on a trumpet. It would be simply a matter of uttering noises into the air (14:7–9). The gift of tongues is therefore limited because it is the only one which requires a companion gift (the gift of interpretation or translation). It is the only one which cannot build up the church on its own. Without an interpretation, the public use of tongues turns everyone else in the church into a *barbaros* or 'foreigner' (14:11) i.e. someone who has no idea of the meaning of the language. It is therefore more limited than the rest of the gifts, and should not be over-emphasized. Even in the private use of tongues, a believer needs to pray for the gift of interpretation, 'For this reason the man who speaks in a tongue should pray that he may interpret what he says' (14:13).

4. Another limitation of this gift revolves around its 'non-rational' character. Paul says that the mind is 'unfruitful' when we use the gift of tongues (14:14). The mental processes which are usually required in any normal act of communication are dormant in the case of tongues-speaking. This does not mean that *glossolalia* is an ecstatic phenomenon in which we are lifted out of our minds into a kind of trance-like state. Rather, most commentators describe a kind of spectrum of tongue-speaking, ranging from the 'hot' to the 'cold'. In the 'hot' version, the one who speaks in a tongue is so filled with a desire to worship that he can barely resist the urge to speak in tongues. In the 'cold' version, the person is fully in control. As one popular writer has put it:

> The myth is still perpetuated that the gift of tongues is 'ecstatic' ... We have complete control over the phenomenon. This is why tongues can be suppressed. We can adjust the volume and vary the speed.[6]

However, whether the intensity of the glossalic act is 'hot' or 'cold', Paul still says that the mind is 'unfruitful', and that he would rather speak five words with his mind (i.e. intelligible words) than ten thousand words in a tongue (14:19).

5. Another limitation of this gift has to do with its potential for disorder in public worship. Evidently there was charismatic chaos in the Corinthian gatherings. People who had the gift of tongues were speaking out as soon as they felt the impulse to do so. There were no restrictions on the number of tongues at any given meeting, and there was no requirement that a public tongue should be interpreted. The resulting cacophany was dishonouring to God – who is a God of peace not of confusion – and a bad witness to outsiders. *Glossolalia* is therefore limited because of its potential for chaos. Without wise and proper leadership, worship meetings can turn into a bedlam of unruly, Dionysian behaviour.

6. A final limitation in the area of this gift relates to its potential for confusion. In my opinion, many of the Corinthian believers practised a kind of pagan version of *glossolalia* before they became Christian under Paul's ministry. Paul writes in 1 Corinthians 12:2 that 'you know that when you were pagans, somehow or other you were influenced and led astray by mute idols'. The words 'influenced' and 'led astray' imply an uncontrolled abandonment to spiritual ecstasy. As Ralph Martin puts it:

> Probably the allusion is to the worship of Apollo who was regarded as 'seizing' his devotees and inducing in them a frenzied trance, like the Sibyl of Cumae.[7]

Recent scholarship has revealed that the Oracle at Delphi (the centre of Apollo worship) involved a religious rite in which a young priestess would fall into a state of frenzy and speak out unrecognizable words. These words were then translated into Greek and given as an oracle to the one who sought the will of the gods. If that is right, then clearly there was, in the Corinthian situation, the potential for confusion; it was possible to confuse Christian *glossolalia* with other, non-Christian equivalents. Today, this kind of confusion is even more of a danger. Scholars who have studied tongues-speech report that it is used in a variety of non-Christian contexts. Spittler has identified the following:

Dramatic glossolalia. This occurs primarily in comedy, when actors invent unknown languages for comic effect.

Spiritualistic glossolalia. This is the apparently ecstatic utterance of the spiritualistic medium.

Pathological glossolalia. People affected by drugs, neurological damage, psychotic disorders, can speak in sounds that resemble unknown languages.

Pagan glossolalia. At the time of Paul, there were pagan religions in which a form of *glossolalia* was practised.[8]

So the potential for confusion is there. Today there are many non-Christian versions of *glossolalia*. Carlyle May's important research has uncovered a widespread occurrence of contemporary, pagan forms of *glossolalia*, ranging from 'mumbles and grunts through esoteric priestly languages and imitations of animal speech to widely related instances of *xenolalia*.[9] May has found this phenomenon in Malaysia, Indonesia, Siberia, Arctic regions, China, Japan, Korea, Arabia and Burma. To be sure, it occurs infrequently, but the fact that it occurs at all reveals that there are non-Christian equivalents to the *charisma* of 'speaking in different kinds of tongues'. It also reveals the potential for confusion.

Paul's ambivalence concerning speaking in different kinds of tongues is therefore real and substantial. On the one hand, he is very positive about *glossolalia*, for reasons which we will explore in a moment. He even expresses his wish that all could speak in tongues (though not, of course, at the same time!). However, he is also thoroughly realistic about the limitations of this gift if it is wrongly understood and wrongly used. As we have seen, Paul at least hints at the following limitations.

1   *Glossolalia* can become the source of division, when those who have the gift turn it into a token of true spirituality.
2   *Glossolalia* can evoke ridicule and disdain from unbelievers, who will regard it as an example of religious 'mania'.
3   *Glossolalia* cannot build up the Church on its own (*oikodome*). It is the only *charisma* which needs a companion gift to do that (the gift of interpretation).
4   *Glossolalia* involves the mind being dormant whilst the spirit is active. As such it is a non-rational or supra-rational phenomenon.
5   *Glossolalia*, if not handled in a biblical and responsible way, can result in charismatic anarchy in public worship.
6   *Glossolalia* can be confused with pagan versions of the same thing. It is possible for an unbeliever to confuse it with pagan *glossolalia*, and it is also possible for Christians to mistake pagan *glossolalia* for the gift of tongues.

The Blessings of Tongues

At this point you may well be thinking, 'This is a formidable argument for not using *glossolalia* in any Christian context whatsoever'. After all, the six limitations identified above would seem to most people to be reason enough for discouraging Christians from speaking in tongues. However, it is highly significant that Paul does not take this line. For Paul, abuse is no excuse for disuse. In other words, the fact that the gift of tongues was misused and even abused is no reason for scrapping this *charisma* from the list of the gifts and saying 'no' to its use in church. Far from it! Paul's approach is to correct the wrong use of the gift, and then to outline its right use. If the gift is handled in a right and responsible manner – i.e. for the edification of the Church – then it will be of great blessing. This means, first and foremost, a restriction on the number of people giving a tongue in a worship service. Secondly, it means a regulation concerning the interpretation of a public utterance in tongues:

> If anyone speaks in a tongue, two – or at the most three – should speak, one at a time, and someone must interpret.
>
> (1 Corinthians 14:27)

If these restrictions and regulations are observed, Paul indicates that *glossolalia* will be for the strengthening of the Church (*oikodome*, 1 Corinthians 14:26). For that reason he writes, 'Do not forbid speaking in tongues' (14:39).

Having said that, the gift of tongues is used in two different contexts. There is the public context of Christian worship, and there the blessing comes when the number of glossolalic utterances is restricted to two or three, and where each is interpreted by another. But Paul writes that there is another context for this gift, the context of private prayer. Indeed, he suggests that this is the primary context. 'He who speaks in a tongue,' says Paul, 'edifies himself.' The private expression of the gift of tongues is an act of intimate communication between the believer and God. The public expression is that same act of intimate communication, only shared with the Church. It is within the private context that the blessings of the gift of tongues are most marked and apparent. Here are a few of the many benefits of the private use of tongues.

1. If the believers are able to use the language of the angels (*angelolalia*), then that means we can have something of a foretaste of our eternal home in the here and now. Every time we use the gift of tongues in our personal adoration of God, we experience for a moment 'the presence of the future'. Thus, the gift of tongues is an eschatological gift. It gives a brief sense of the 'not yet' of the kingdom of God. It is a form of prayerful communion in which the 'mysteries' of heaven are enjoyed in the human soul.

2. The private use of tongues is said to be 'edifying'. At the purely psychological level, this has been proved to be the case. Whereas

in early research, *glossolalia* was associated with madness, today it is said to give people a sense of balance, wholeness and well-being.

> Depression among glossolalics is reduced; they become more open to feeling and to the affective dimension of their experience, more spontaneous and better able to cope with anxiety. [10]

At the spiritual level, the gift is edifying because it helps the believer to enjoy a greater intimacy with God. When I speak in tongues in my private prayer life, I commune alone with God. For me, as for many, the gift is the highest form of love-talk with the Father. Indeed, most people who have received the gift of tongues say that it revolutionizes personal prayer.

3.   The gift of tongues is a blessing because there are many times when verbal prayer is simply inadequate to express our deepest thanksgiving and praise. Paul says, in 1 Corinthians 14:16, that *glossolalia* expresses *eucharistia* (gratitude) and *eulogia* (praise and adoration). Sometimes we catch a glimpse of the indescribable depths of the Infinite God. At times like these, words are simply not enough to express our devotion. At those moments, *glossolalia* (or, more accurately, *angelolalia*) enables the believer to transcend the poverty of human language. For those who struggle with articulating their thoughts, this is a liberating, inclusive and truly democratic gift.

4.   The gift of tongues releases a greater sense of the Spirit's presence in our lives. As we learn to use this gift, the sense of the reality of 'God's empowering presence' grows stronger in our hearts. Furthermore, the presence of this gift in a believer's life makes it possible to pray throughout the day. Those who enjoy the gift of tongues can live in a continuous stream of prayer and 'practise the presence of God', whatever context or circumstance they may find themselves in.

5.   The gift of tongues is an expression of the deepest kind of joy. This is particularly true with 'singing in tongues'. Many Christians spend a good deal of their private devotions praying and singing in tongues. This has opened up a whole new vista of prayerful

worship. Indeed, private prayer is never boring when it involves this level of intimacy with God. Prayer becomes less rigid and more spontaneous. It enables us to minister to the Lord with far greater passion and power.

6.   The gift of tongues gives us a sense of continuity with the earliest Christian Church. No longer is there a great divide between the experience of the first Christians and ourselves. Now, with the release of this gift in our lives, we can enjoy something of the immediacy of God which was enjoyed by the believers in the New Testament churches.

7.   The gift of tongues helps us to yield more to the Spirit. In Western culture, we have learnt how to be 'in control' in every conceivable situation. This has resulted in a form of Christianity in which God is rarely allowed to take total charge of our lives. As somebody once said,

> In all Christians, Christ is present
> In some Christians, Christ is prominent
> In few Christians, Christ is pre-eminent

Speaking in tongues is helpful because it enables us to yield more to the control of the Spirit. A far greater abandonment to God is made possible whenever we surrender our speech organs and our control of language to the power of the Spirit.

So, while there are a number of limitations to this gift (particularly in the public domain), as an aid to private prayer *glossolalia* has enormous value. No wonder Paul exercised this gift so frequently in his own life, declaring that he used it more than all the Corinthians (1 Corinthians 14:18).

Tongues for Every Believer?

Many classical Pentecostals have taken the position that every Christian should receive the gift of tongues when she or he is filled with the Holy Spirit for the first time (i.e. when they are baptized in the Spirit). I do not personally share this view that tongues is the evidence of true initiation into the kingdom of God, my own opinion being that the restriction of 'initial evidence' to *glossolalia* is not true to Scripture. As I have argued elsewhere, the primary indication that a person has been filled with the Holy Spirit is 'inspired speech',[11] and this can take a variety of forms: prophesying, speaking in tongues, praising God, proclaiming the Gospel, and so on. In other words, what pours out of a person is a sign of what has been poured in. If it is the Spirit which has been poured in to us, then it will be 'charismatic speech' which pours out. That may be *glossolalia*, but it need not necessarily be. It could be almost any kind of bold, uninhibited speech.

My own view is therefore this: not every Christian receives the gift of tongues when he or she is filled with the Holy Spirit for the first time. Some do, and where they are 'surprised by joy' in this way, it is a wonderful blessing. However, not everyone receives this gift. Paul says as much. He asks:

Are all apostles?
Are all prophets?
Are all teachers?
Do all work miracles?
Do all have the gifts of healing?
Do all speak in tongues?
Do all interpret?

In each of these cases, the answer is 'no'. Thus, the attempt to interpret Paul's question above to the public exercise of *glossolalia* is invalid. 1 Corinthians 12 is about the gifts of the Spirit, and the only gift which Paul says all believers can have is prophecy. Paul may therefore say, 'I would like every one of you to speak in tongues' (1 Corinthians 14:5), but the fact remains: *glossolalia* is a grace-gift of the Spirit, and like all the grace-gifts bar prophecy, it is given to some members of the Body of Christ, but not to all.

Having said that, the gift of tongues is one which all should desire. As Wayne Grudem has said,

> There is nothing in Scripture that says only a few will receive the gift of speaking in tongues, and since it is a gift which Paul views as edifying and useful in prayer and worship (on a personal level even if not in church), it would not be surprising if the Holy Spirit gave a very wide distribution of this gift and many Christians in fact received it.[11]

In my own pastoral ministry, I therefore encourage every believer to pray for this gift, and to pray 'in faith' – i.e. believing that God will give what they do not yet experience and use. Many have received this gift, and many continue to receive it. Some receive it on their own as they pray to God. Others receive it when hands are laid upon them and others pray for the gift to be imparted. Some receive it as they worship God in privacy. Others receive it as they are worshipping God in a meeting where the atmosphere is thick with angels. There is seemingly no end to the various ways used by God to give this gift to his children. So do not despair and give up if you do not receive it straightaway. As Jesus said, in the context of the Father's good gifts,

> Go on asking, and you will receive
> Go on seeking, and you will find
> Go on knocking, and the door will be opened. (Matthew 7:7)

Questions

1 Is this a gift which you have received?
2 What are the personal benefits of this gift in your life?
3 If you have not yet received this gift, what are you going to do now?
4 Is this gift used in corporate worship in your church?
5 How is the gift handled in that context?
6 Have you ever heard of, or witnessed, an example of *xenolalia*?
7 Do you think every Christian should have the gift of tongues?
8 What is your view about tongues as 'initial evidence'?

9   How has this chapter increased your understanding of this gift?
10 If you have been hurt by the use of this gift, how are you going to
    deal with that in future?

Prayer

Dear Lord Jesus, I simply ask that you would give me the gift of
tongues. Release this anointing in my life, so that I can praise you in
uninhibited intimacy. Bless the Church with this gift, good Lord. Help
us to use it wisely and well, so that every member of the Body of Christ
may be edified. Protect us from divisive attitudes, and forgive us for any
insensitive use of this precious anointing. So come, Holy Spirit. I ask
for more power and joy in my prayer life, and in the life of the Church.
Send the fire of Pentecost, and ignite our hearts with a fervent passion
for you. Help us to express our adoration in the language of angels, and
let there be a constant stream of praise from our hearts and voices.
These things I humbly ask, in your name. Amen.

NINE

The Interpretation of Tongues

We come now to the last of the grace-gifts of the Spirit listed by Paul in 1 Corinthians 12:8–10. Paul writes, 'to another [is given] the interpretation of tongues'. This is the most neglected of all the gifts of the Spirit. The main reason for this is because it is the only gift which does not stand on its own. Paul says that the gift of interpretation is concerned with 'tongues'. Consequently, the gift of the interpretation of tongues is not the supernatural ability to interpret dreams, pictures and other visual phenomena. The evaluation of 'revelation' is the province of 'the discernings of spirits'. Rather, we need to note Paul's precise wording, that this gift is the 'interpretation *of tongues*', that is to say, the ability to translate a public, *glossolalic* utterance into the vernacular of the congregation. As Rod Williams puts it:

> This gift is not interpretation in general but functions only in relation to tongues. All the other gifts, though closely related, are independent manifestations of the Holy Spirit. However, there is no spiritual gift of interpretation as such; rather, the gift is only that of interpretation of tongues.[1]

It is because the gift of interpretation exists in a dependent relationship with speaking in different kinds of tongues that it is so often neglected. However, this is really a mistake. A genuine demonstration of the gift of interpretation is as extraordinary and as miraculous as a genuine example of charismatic healing. The gift of interpretation, like all the gifts, is not a human ability but a charismatic and inspired ability. In this respect, it is important right at the outset to distinguish it from what goes on at international conferences. At the United Nations, for example, delegates from every country sit with headsets on, and an expert interpreter translates each of the speeches straight-away into their native languages. This ability to translate a language immediately, impressive though it is, is still a natural, human, learnt ability. This is likewise the case in Christian conferences. When I go to Norway and speak to members of the Norwegian churches, my words are translated by a wonderful man of God called Bjorn. Bjorn himself would say that his ability to translate my words is both human and fallible. Indeed, last year he made a marvellous mistranslation of the following statement:

If a leader wants his people to bleed, then he must be prepared to haemorrhage.

Bjorn mistranslated that as,

If a leader wants his people to bleed, then he must be prepared to have haemorrhoids!

Needless to say, a lot of pastors were shuffling rather uncomfortably in their seats at this point!

The gift of interpretation of tongues is therefore not the same thing as the human ability to translate foreign languages. This is even the case when God chooses to communicate revelation in a language which is no longer in use (a dead language). I have come across one or two examples of this, though they are very rare. This particular phenomenon usually involves a believer seeing something written in an ancient language which then has to be translated. A woman in a church near mine had an experience of precisely this last year. She saw a paragraph of what turned out to be New Testament Greek which she then wrote down and passed to her vicar. Her vicar handed them on to me, and with the help of some Greek scholars,

(Wow!

we translated the paragraph. It contained a number of Scriptural quotations, followed by an exhortation to welcome and not despise the person who had written down the message. The remarkable thing about this incident is that the woman in question (who has a good track record in hearing God) has very little education and has never seen New Testament Greek, let alone written it. Consequently, while the actual language of the revelation was possibly inspired by the Holy Spirit, its interpretation was not. It was purely a matter of a group of Greek scholars getting together and using their acquired knowledge to offer an exact translation of the message.

A similar incident to this is recorded by Timothy Pain in his little book entitled, *Tongues and Explanations*. He writes:

> During the August 1970 meeting, an evangelical Anglican lady received a vision of written words in what was to her an unknown tongue. In her mind she saw a cross with the words, *Stat crux dum volvitur orbis*, inscribed over the top. She was uncertain what to do as spiritual gifts were then unknown in public meetings at Ashburnham. So she wrote it down and sought out the local vicar in the tea interval.[2]

The vicar realized that this word was in Latin, and translated it as 'The cross stands while the world revolves'. This translation was read out at the next meeting, and aroused considerable interest. Six weeks later, a local lay reader discovered that this Latin phrase was the centuries old motto of the Carthusian monks.

In both of these examples, there is a case to be made out for the 'charismatic' nature of the revelation involved. I am aware of the existence of something similar to this in modern spiritualism. The ability to write something in a dead or living language is, in that context, referred to as *xenographia*. While there may well be a case for a psychological (particularly a Jungian) understanding of the incidents described above, I would be reluctant to ascribe them to psychic *xenographia*. It seems to me that there is biblical precedent for this kind of phenomenon, particularly in the story of Daniel and King Belshazzar (Daniel 5:1–31). During a sumptuous feast, a hand appears from nowhere and writes some words on the wall of the palace. Belshazzar is frightened and mystified, so he eventually summons Daniel and says,

> I have heard that the spirit of the gods is in you and that you have insight, intelligence and outstanding wisdom. The wise men and enchanters were brought before me to read this writing and tell me what it means, but they could not explain it. Now I have heard that you are able to give interpretations and to solve difficult problems. If you can read this writing and tell me what it means, you will be clothed in purple and have a gold chain placed around your neck, and you will be made the third highest ruler in the kingdom (5:14–16).

Daniel tells Belshazzar to keep his gifts, and then offers a translation of the words on the wall: *MENE, MENE, TEKEL, PARSIN.*

> *Mene*: God has numbered the days of your reign and brought it to an end.

> *Tekel*: You have been weighed on the scales and found wanting.

> *Peres*: Your kingdom is divided and given to the Medes and the Persians.[3]

In this example, the writing on the wall is a supernatural work. The interpretation is not. The words on the wall are written by God, but they are written in Aramaic, which was Daniel's native language. Daniel's interpretation was therefore not a matter of inspired translation, it was merely a matter of translating something in his own language into the mother tongue of King Belshazzar. Thus, the writing on the wall in Daniel 5 was an instance of divine *xenographia*. There is therefore some biblical precedent for this phenomenon. For this reason, I am hesitant about dismissing the modern-day examples cited above.

The Need for Interpretation

The point needs stressing at the outset: when Paul speaks of the interpretation of tongues, he is not speaking of a natural, learnt, human ability. He is speaking about a charismatic, inspired and indeed miraculous phenomenon. He is alluding to

> *the special, charismatic ability to translate a public utterance of* glosso-lalia *into the vernacular of the congregation.*

It is important at this juncture to understand what I mean by *glossolalia*. In the last chapter on 'different kinds of tongues' we distinguished between two main kinds of *glossolalia* or tongue-speech: the first was *xenolalia*, and I defined that as

> *the supernatural, spontaneous ability to speak in unlearnt human lang-uages, in such a way that the wonders of God are heard and understood by those for whom these languages are the native dialect.*

When someone gives a *xenolalic* utterance in church today, the one for whom this utterance is intended does not require the charis-matic gift of interpretation in order to understand it. The reason for this is because *xenolalia* is a miracle of speech not a miracle of hearing. It is the charismatic ability to speak in an unlearnt foreign language in such a way that a foreigner can immediately under-stand what is being said. Thus, at Pentecost, the crowds did not need an interpretation because they heard the disciples speaking in their own languages (*ta idia dialecta*, Acts 2:8). They understood straightaway what was being said, though the disciples themselves might have appreciated a translation!

The examples of *xenolalia* in recent church history further con-firm the fact that this particular form of *glossolalia* does not need interpretation by the recipient of the message. During a recent lec-ture course on 'The Holy Spirit in the New Testament', one of my students unearthed a number. Here are a few:

An example of speaking in foreign tongues which led to evangelization has been told by William Caldwell, a Pentecostal evangelist, in the booklet *Pentecostal Baptism*. During a revival crusade he conducted in southern California a few years ago, the pastor of the local church spoke in tongues when a rabbinical student who had worked on a co-operative farm in Israel was present. The young Jew immediately identified the speech as fluent Hebrew, which he understood clearly, and the young man was himself convinced by the power of this evidence.

Last week a woman arose during the meeting and spoke for ten minutes, no one apparently in the audience knowing what she said. An Indian who had come from the Pawnee Reservation in the territory that day to attend the services, stated that she was speaking in the language of his tribe and that he could understand every word of the testimony.

On one occasion, when Father Regimbal sang in tongues, an elderly Baptist pastor broke down in tears and said, 'The song you were singing is a Hebrew Christian song from the fourth century. When I was a student in Jerusalem, this was one of the songs used to prove that there had been a Christian community in Jerusalem at that time. It's a song about the Prince of Peace. You used the words and music I learnt in Jerusalem.'

In each of these instances, the form of *glossolalia* seems to have been *xenolalia*. In the first and second examples, the utterance was intended for a foreigner in the congregation. In all three cases, the gift of interpretation was not required because the utterance was in the mother tongue of the intended recipient. Therefore, in the case of the public use of *xenolalia*, there is no need for the gift of interpretation. The one who understands the message in his own mother tongue simply stands and announces to the congregation that the utterance was in a particular language, and then, if appropriate, shares a translation.

In the case of the second form of *glossolalia*, however, the gift of interpretation is required. You will recall from chapter 8 that we followed Paul in distinguishing between the tongues of men (*xenolalia*) and the tongues of angels (*angelolalia*). I followed the example of a number of Bible teachers who see the latter as the main focus of Paul's instructions in 1 Corinthians 14. In that chapter, Paul is referring to the public use of *glossolalia* in the church assembly. The particular form of *glossolalia* to which he is referring is primarily 'the tongues of angels'. When we speak in tongues in our private devotions, that tongue speaking is usually *angelolalia* not *xenolalia*. It is the transcendent, heavenly language of adoration used by the angels. Sometimes, in the context of public worship, the Holy Spirit prompts us to use that same gift. We then utter in public something of what the Spirit inspires us to say in private. Whenever that occurs, Paul says that there must be an interpretation. When a true interpretation is offered, this is 'a miracle of hearing'. It is not the human ability to translate a foreign language (*xenographia/xenolalia*). It is the supra-human, inspired ability to translate the language of the angels. In my estimation, this gift is every bit as extraordinary, impressive and supernatural as the ability to heal the sick, pronounce God's mind, exorcize demons, and raise the dead. It is a miracle indeed.

The Nature of Interpretation

It is this charismatic ability to interpret public *angelolalia* which Paul is referring to when he writes, 'to another [is given] the interpretation of tongues'. The word translated 'interpretation' is the Greek word *hermeneia*, from which we get the technical term 'hermeneutics', meaning 'the art of interpreting literature'. In ancient Greek, *hermeneia* simply means a 'translation'. Paul says in 1 Corinthians 14:2 that the glossalist speaks 'mysteries' to God in his spirit. In other words, he speaks 'mysteries of which only the angels in heaven have knowledge'. As James Dunn puts it:

> Paul thus characterizes the glossalist as holding a secret conversation with God (he speaks to God: 14:2); the subject matter is the eschatological secrets known only in heaven; so presumably the language used is the language of heaven. (Revelation 14:2f.)[4]

When someone utters this kind of *glossolalia* in public, it stands to reason that an inspired *hermeneia* or 'interpretation' will be required.

All this points to the value and the necessity of the charism of interpretation when anyone utters *angelolalia* in public. What actually happens when someone operates in this particular gift? In the context of public worship, the process begins when someone stands and speaks in tongues. Normally there are several people in a Charismatic or a Pentecostal church who have ministered quite regularly in the gift of interpretation. At this point, one of them will receive revelation from the Holy Spirit as to the meaning of the utterance. This need not necessarily be a 'word-for-word' translation; it may just be the gist of the meaning of the utterance. In other words, there is probably a spectrum from literal translation at one end, to general paraphrase at the other. For this reason, an interpretation may be longer or shorter than the length of the glossolalic utterance. Whatever the length, a genuine interpretation will provide what Rod Williams calls 'the valuable content of what has been spoken in a tongue'.[5] When this occurs, everyone in the church can add their 'Amen' to the utterance (1 Corinthians 14:16), and the Body of Christ can be strengthened and encouraged (14:5).

The gift of interpretation is accordingly a supernatural ability to render the essence of a glossalic utterance in the vernacular of the congregation. The word *hermeneia* (translated 'interpretation') covers a wide range of possibilities. As Russell Spittler says, it ranges

> From 'speech' that expresses what is unclear, through 'translation' that exchanges from one language to another, to 'commentary' that explains or interprets … But in all the uses of the word, the movement from obscurity or unintelligibility to clarity of expression prevails.[6]

Thus, genuine interpretation will result not in confusion but in clarity. In this respect, we should remember that the natural ability to translate foreign languages is fallible. I well remember visiting an aquarium in Majorca, where statements about each of the species were printed next to each tank. These had clearly been translated through at least four languages before they were eventually rendered in English. Some of the results were almost nonsensical:

> The most of fresh water fish are gregarian, it means they are always agrupated or in covey.
>
> This species is from Indo-Pacific ocean and poison of their bone can be mortal. Between the corals of the reefs a large number of specimens pollulate and they hid fastly when they assume peril.
>
> Electrophorus Electricus. May mido 3m and produces electric unburdening up to 800V!

Needless to say a genuine interpretation of *glossolalia* will not leave us with this level of confusion. What is unintelligible will be made intelligible.

As for the 'valuable content' of the utterance, we should remember the point made in the last chapter; the interpretation will usually be rendered in the form of a prayer of thanksgiving or praise. In other words, it will be translated in the form of a Godward statement, not a prophetic word from God to the Church. There is a widespread assumption in Charismatic and Pentecostal churches that the interpretation of a tongue is a word of prophecy. Most people accept the equation $T + I = P$; in other words, Tongues + Interpretation = Prophecy. However, the exegetical support for this view is non-existent. Paul says that *glossolalia* is directed towards God, not to man:

> The one speaking in a tongue speaks not to human beings but to God.
>
> (1 Corinthians 14:2)

He speaks out 'mysteries' in the language of the angels. Thus, when a tongue is given in public, there is a sense in which the congregation is 'overhearing' the passionate worship of an individual believer. If an interpretation is offered which is not in the form of prayerful adoration, we should be cautious about regarding it as a genuine interpretation. If it is offered in the form of praise language, then it has a much better chance of being the true 'interpretation', as the following incident illustrates:[7]

On Sunday, 31 March 1985, Lyn Pain, the minister's wife and leader of the music, sang a solo song in tongues in the course of evening worship. Her husband, Alan, who was leading the service at the time, felt that he had received the explanation of this tongue and, somewhat tentatively, offered it in the form of a prayer.

However, many in the congregation did not realize that this prayer had been given as the explanation to the tongue, and a few minutes later, towards the end of the service, a lady came to the front. She read out an explanation, which she had written down, to the song sung earlier in tongues. Its harmony with Alan's explanation was striking and, on impulse, Alan asked the congregation to sit down.

He informed them that his earlier prayer had been intended as the explanation, commented on the marked similarity between the two explanations, and then asked any others who had had a similar 'impression' to raise a hand. Between fifteen and twenty people raised a hand. There were men and woman of all stages of Christian experience.

Alan was thus able to show them that they had not merely had an impression, but had received from the Lord the charismatic gift of 'explanation'. It was an extremely valuable opportunity to encourage them to boldness for the future, and also a uniquely valuable object lesson for the whole church, especially those who were wary because they had felt that these things lacked any spiritual objectivity.

This story highlights the fact that the interpretation of a public tongue should generally be in the form of a prayer of adoration. In this matter, I therefore part company from many of my Charismatic and Pentecostal friends. In my opinion, even a Bible scholar as able as Rod Williams, gets this wrong:

It is sometimes said that since in a tongue one speaks not to men but to God, the interpretation following must likewise be addressed to God. Hence there can be no message to people ... This viewpoint, I submit, is mistaken.[8]

However, I believe Williams is the one who is mistaken here. I cannot see why God would choose to bring a revelation to the Church by means of a tongue and an interpretation when he could bring it in the much more simple and direct form of a prophecy. It makes no sense to me for a person to bring a prophetic revelation in the form of a tongue plus an interpretation. It makes a lot of sense that God would cause us to be edified by overhearing some words of extra-ordinary praise which are first uttered in the form of *angelolalia*, and then translated miraculously into the vernacular. Even Rod Williams makes this point:

> If tongues plus interpretation equals prophecy, I submit, there would be no need for the former two. Why bother about these two gifts (with their complexity) when one gift will do equally well?[9]

Exactly! Tongues plus Interpretation equals Praise, not Prophecy!

If I may speak personally for a moment, I regularly use the gift of tongues in my private devotional life. I find it an indispensable aid to thanksgiving and praise, especially when I lack the human words for what to say to God. On one occasion, during a half-night of prayer in church, I felt compelled by the Spirit to speak this same language in public. A sister who has the gift of interpretation gave the following rendition of my words:

> You are my Father. You pour out your blessings upon me like silver rain and I love you. I love you with all of my heart, my dearest Papa.

The moment she uttered these words, I knew that they were the correct translation. I knew that in my mind, because it conformed to the teaching of Paul about 'interpretation'. I knew it in my spirit, because I felt an immediate sense of 'this is right!' The effect on the worship that night was electric. The effects in my own personal devotions have been incredibly enriching. Truly,

$$T + I = P$$

Tongues plus Interpretation = Praise.

The Number of Interpretations

In a public act of worship, Paul is very firm about the number of glossalic utterances. He says that two, or at the most three, people should be allowed to speak in tongues. After each tongue, an interpretation should be given by one person (1 Corinthians 14:27). More than that, if people who speak in tongues know that one who has the gift of interpretation is absent, they should refrain from speaking in tongues at all. What these words reveal is that there were believers in Corinth who were known to have the gift of interpretation. This is why Paul can say 'Do all interpret tongues?' (1 Corinthians 12:30). The answer is 'no'. Why? Because only some are anointed to offer interpretations of tongues. Interpretation, like the gifts in general, is given to some but not to all. Paul therefore teaches that the public use of *glossolalia* is dependent upon the presence of a charismatic interpreter in the worship gathering. If an interpreter is absent, then public *glossolalia* has the same value as a music group playing indiscernible harmonies, or a bugler playing an incomprehensible noise (as was going on, apparently, in Corinth).

From this evidence we can see that Paul accords far more value to the gift of interpretation than we do today. Here are a few likely reasons why. First, for Paul the gift of interpretation was probably the perfect illustration of the Church as a Body with many interdependent parts. When someone interpreted a tongue correctly, this highlighted the fact that the different parts of the Body of Christ cannot despise one another, let alone do without each other. Secondly, for Paul the gift of interpretation was evidence of what he called 'the fellowship of the Holy Spirit'. The fact that one person could understand the meaning of another's *glossolalia* was wonderful evidence of the *koinonia* which the Holy Spirit brings. This was especially true in those cases when a person came to church with an interpretation of a tongue *which had not yet been spoken out by another* (a phenomenon which Paul seems to imply in 1 Corinthians 14:26). Thirdly, for Paul the gift of interpretation was essential for maintaining order in worship. The fact that each public tongue had to be interpreted meant that there were some 'brakes' in charismatic worship. Interpretation sometimes takes time, and this fact alone minimizes the risk of glossolalic chaos. It reduces the possibility of public worship turning into a cacophanous stream of untranslated *glossolalia*.

So, there is good sense in Paul's appreciation for this gift, and indeed in his restrictions concerning the number of tongues and interpretations in public worship. One question remains, however. How does this apply to the common practice of 'singing in tongues'? Obviously this was a phenomenon known to Paul, because he writes about singing with one's spirit in 1 Corinthians 14:15–16. Did Paul expect 'singing in tongues' to be interpreted? My own feeling is that Paul would have expected a glossolalic song to be interpreted if it was sung as a solo, but that he would not have expected an interpretation if the whole congregation had been singing in tongues. In the second scenario, everyone is basically praising God in the tongue which they use in private. Since the interpretations of each of these private tongues may vary, it is impractical to demand that a corporate time of sung *glossolalia* should be translated. The best thing is for the leader to say something along these lines:

> Lord, we thank you so much for that marvellous expression of spiritual adoration. You know what we were each of us singing, and we worship you for that. Please accept our praises, and thank you, Lord, for the language of the angels, and indeed for enabling us to join in with the angels. In your precious name. Amen.

So, as far as corporate singing in tongues is concerned, the gift of interpretation seems largely irrelevant. I am not persuaded by those who say that corporate, sung *glossolalia* should be interpreted because everyone is singing the same song in their spirits. That is not borne out by Paul's teaching in 1 Corinthians 14, even if it is suggested by Luke's report of the *xenolalia* in Acts 2. However, we have seen already in this chapter that Paul is talking about angel-tongues not foreign languages. So corporate singing in the spirit does not need to be interpreted; solo singing, however, does. This interpretation can be offered in a number of ways:

1 The singer includes both angelic words and their translation in the song itself.
2 The singer sings a song in tongues, then sings the same song in the vernacular.
3 The singer sings the song in tongues, and then someone with the gift of interpretation either sings or speaks out the meaning of the song.

Thus, in the case of solo singing the really important thing is that there is an interpretation.

The Nurture of Interpretation

One of the things we have discovered in this book is that some of our understanding of the gifts of the Spirit is influenced more by experience than by exegesis. This has proved to be especially true in the case of the word of knowledge, but it is also true in the case of tongues and interpretation. In this chapter we have studied the biblical teaching on these two, complementary gifts, and the results have been, in some cases, surprising. They have revealed the need for a number of correctives to the current popular understanding of tongues and interpretation. These need to be made if the two gifts are to be properly nurtured in the Church. If tongues and interpretation are to be the joyous gifts which the Father designed them to be, then we must be sure to let Scripture mould experience rather than vice versa. Our experience of the gifts can greatly help to refine our understanding of Scripture. But it must not be allowed to take precedence over what Scripture teaches, either implicitly or explicitly. With that in mind, let me suggest several refinements to the traditional Pentecostal and Charismatic practice of these gifts.

1. We must put an end once and for all to the view that missionaries to foreign lands do not need to learn the languages of those nations because they can rely on the Holy Spirit to give them *xenolalic* utterances, as in Acts 2. This view, associated with the early Pentecostal pioneer and pastor, Charles Parham, cannot be sustained

from Scripture. I do believe that there are exceptional circumstances on the mission field when God gives the gift of *xenolalia* to a missionary. When H.B. Goulock, for example, was confronted by a group of hostile cannibals in the Pahn territory of Africa in 1922, he was miraculously enabled to speak their own language. Another example is that of Tommy Hicks. Some years ago in Russia, his interpreter suddenly left him. Hicks prayed, and the Holy Spirit enabled him to speak in the language of the people who were listening. So, *xenolalia* does happen. However, it is the exception rather than the rule. The excesses of the Parham school must be avoided. While remaining open to the miracle of *xenolalia* in rare circumstances, it seems to me that the more pragmatic approach is to take the trouble to learn the language of the people concerned!

2. The notion that a tongue can be interpreted as a prophecy needs to be revised. As I have already indicated, the Pauline view is that tongues-speaking is a Godward not a manward mode of prayerful address. Yet, as James Dunn points out in a footnote in *Jesus and the Spirit*,

> In the twentieth-century Pentecostal and charismatic movements the interpretation of a tongue has often sounded more like a prophecy than the interpretation of a prayer.[10]

It would be helpful if church leaders stressed this right from the start in Charismatic churches. When Paul says that the one speaking in tongues to God 'utters mysteries', this does not mean 'secret words of revelation' which are then to be communicated to the Church. It simply means that the glossolalist utters mysterious things, which is manifestly the case.

3. If these gifts are to be responsibly nurtured in the Church, people should be encouraged to value the gift of interpretation. It seems to me that this is the most neglected of all the gifts, yet there are few things more miraculous than the supernatural ability to convey the meaning of either one's own *glossolalia*, or that of someone else in public worship. It is incredibly affirming and moving to have

one's own tongues-speech translated. It is just as powerful to hear someone else offering the same interpretation which the Spirit has laid on your heart as well. If the gift of interpretation is to be properly nurtured in the Church, then we need a higher view of the gift. When an interpreter is around, a tongue is miraculously translated into the vernacular. When that happens, the community of the Spirit is simultaneously embraced by a common 'Amen'. The whole Church is edified when this happens, and frequently the floodgates of truly anointed worship are opened. Without interpretation, none of these things can happen. It is therefore time to give this gift its rightful value.

Paul says that we are to desire the spiritual gifts, especially those which edify the Church (the 'higher gifts'). When tongues is accompanied by interpretation, then it becomes one such 'higher gift'. When it is not, then it lacks any real value. No wonder, then, that it is so important to pray for 'the interpretation of tongues'. In that respect, though I have disagreed with Williams' views on the content of an interpretation, I am happy to agree with him on the importance of interpretation. He writes:

> Without interpretation spiritual tongues must remain silent in the gathered community. From all that has been observed about the intrinsic value of tongues, such silence would be a serious loss. Thus interpretation of tongues is a gift of the Spirit earnestly to be desired. 'Earnestly desire the spiritual gifts' (1 Corinthians 14:1) means *all* of them, the last of which (in 1 Corinthians 12:8–10) is interpretation of tongues. Perhaps this gift seems modest when compared with such gifts as healings and miracles (who would not desire them?); moreover, it is dependent on another gift, the gift of 'kinds of tongues', even to function. *Yet* and this is a large 'yet' – interpretation of tongues ... is the key that for the community unlocks the profundity of things that are uttered in the Spirit.[11]

Questions

1 Have you ever used the gift of 'interpretation of tongues'?
2 Is it your experience that a tongue is followed by a prophecy rather than a word of praise?

3   Do you agree that the content of an interpretation should be a word of prayerful adoration or thanksgiving?
4   If you speak in tongues privately, do you ask the Holy Spirit to interpret what you are saying?
5   Have you even been in a context of worship where a tongue has not been interpreted?
6   Have you ever experienced the phenomenon of corporate singing in tongues?
7   Have you ever heard a solo song in tongues without an interpretation?
8   Do you think there is a place for 'tongues' in the realm of intercessory prayer?
9   What is the Biblical support for such a practice?
10 If you do think it is biblical, does such glossolalic utterance need interpreting?

Prayer

Dear Lord, I thank you so much for revealing the great value of the gift of interpretation. I confess that I have neglected this gift in both private and public contexts. Please help me to know what I am praying when I worship you in this precious, non-verbal way. Please help us as a Church to follow tongues with interpretation. Edify the whole Church through the responsible use of tongues and interpretation, O Lord. In your name. Amen.

Conclusion

This book has been a close analysis of the spiritual gifts in 1 Corinthians 12:8–10. My use of the recent studies on these more extraordinary gifts of the Spirit has given us some new perspectives as well as some timely correctives. In the Introduction I mentioned the way in which the popular understanding of these gifts has been influenced too much by experience and not enough by exegesis. Our findings have revealed that in some areas there has been a very obvious misunderstanding of the true nature of certain *charismata*. In this respect, I have, I think, confirmed the view of Siegfried Schatzmann who, at the end of his book entitled *A Pauline Theology of Charismata*, said that 'experience alone is an unreliable and insufficient hermeneutical principle.'[1] However, Schatzmann goes on to add that the same goes for a purely objective study of the gifts. Thus, while the exclusively experiential approach leads to reductionism, so does the exclusively objective, scientific approach. I have therefore attempted to steer a kind of middle course between objective exegesis on the one hand, and subjective experience on the other. No doubt I have sometimes failed to get the balance right, but in spite of my shortcomings, I do hope that this book will encourage those who have no charismatic experience to pray earnestly for the gifts, and those who use little exegesis to get deeper into the Scriptures. That way we may indeed move closer towards that marriage of Word and Spirit which seems to be on the hearts of so many evangelicals today.

The Extraordinary and the Ordinary

Having said that, it is important that I end this book with some comments concerning some of the gifts which Paul does not mention in 1 Corinthians 12:8-10. The gifts which he does allude to are ones which veer towards the sensational end of the charismatic spectrum. Wisdom, knowledge, faith, gifts of healings, miraculous works, prophecy, discernment, different kinds of tongues and interpretation all belong to the more spectacular, extraordinary category of gifts. In Pentecostal and Charismatic circles, it is these gifts which tend to get emphasized more than any other. This has unfortunately resulted in a kind of pneumatic sensationalism in which only the dramatic gifts are ever taught and encouraged. What started out as a laudable attempt to correct the widespread lack of spiritual power and faith-expectancy in the churches has regrettably led in some contexts to a kind of cult of the spectacular. As Michael Welker has recently put it, in his book called *God the Spirit*,

> With the Charismatic Movement the interest in the Holy Spirit seems frequently to concentrate on the unusual, *sensational* action of the Spirit.[2]

Welker puts this down to the enlightened scepticism of the average Western mentality. He sees it as a reaction against the homogeneity, predictability and rationality of Enlightenment culture. Yet, at the same time, he regards the Charismatic interest in subjective, irrational and exotic experiences as a potentially dangerous road. His advice is as follows:

> Instead of busying itself with unusual, sensational actions of the Spirit, a theology of the Holy Spirit ought to work towards an understanding of experiences of the Spirit that are open to sober and realistic perception.[3]

I think Welker is perhaps overstating his case, for our study of the Pauline *charismata* has proved that there are dramatic operations of the Spirit's power, and these need to be seen as a part of the church's worship and mission. Having said that, I cannot help thinking that there is some sense even in Welker's hyperbole. One man who has been a guiding light to the Charismatic movement is Donald Gee, and I have often been struck by his remark that 'many of our errors where spiritual gifts are concerned arise when we want the extraordinary and exceptional to be made the frequent and the habitual'.[4] That is not only well put, it is true. One of the things which causes most tension in a church entering into renewal is the pressure for people to embrace a spirituality focused on the exceptional and the extraordinary. This not only alienates those who feel that their gifts are more ordinary and invisible, it also creates an unhealthy pressure to conform to a way of life which is permanently miraculous. This in turn causes a two-tiered Christianity in which the 'spiritual' ones are speaking in tongues and healing the sick, and the unspiritual ones are merely setting out chairs and serving the coffee. That is the error made in Corinth, and it is sad to have to report that history has often repeated itself on that score.

One of the tasks which remains in this book is therefore that of reinstating the value of what are commonly assumed to be more ordinary gifts. In that regard, we need to begin by recognizing that Paul spoke of the gifts of the Holy Spirit not only as *energemata* (works of power) but as *diakoniai* (acts of service). If we draw up a spectrum of the gifts of the Spirit, we will quickly see that all the gifts can be placed somewhere along a line from the 'extraordinary gifts of power' at one end, to the 'ordinary gifts of service' at the other. In the diagram below, I have put just some of the gifts on this line:

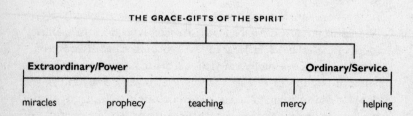

THE GRACE-GIFTS OF THE SPIRIT

Extraordinary/Power   Ordinary/Service

miracles   prophecy   teaching   mercy   helping

The same continuum can be drawn up with different categories – with the gifts which are overtly supernatural at one end (such as tongues and healing), and those which *appear* more natural at the other (such as helping and showing mercy). The important thing to realize, however, is that whatever special ability God has given us, it still comes under the category of what Paul called the *charismata*.

This means that those who tend to stress manifestations such as 'tongues, prophecy and healing', need to have a greater reverence for gifts such as helping, serving and administration. Likewise, those who think only in terms of the more ordinary gifts need to have a greater openness to the more spectacular charisms. To use Paul's body language, the presentable parts need to have a greater respect for the more unpresentable ones, and vice versa. In the pages that remain, I want to spend some time describing and promoting the neglected gifts of the Spirit. In doing that I am mindful of the fact that a whole book could be devoted to these particular charisms. I am also aware that the little space which I am giving them, in contrast to the much greater space given to the more dramatic gifts, will make me vulnerable to the same criticism which I have levelled against others. However, I am prepared to take that risk because I do believe that those who have the gifts below need to feel that they are a valued part of the Church as well. So we will look at two of the 'works of service' described by Paul – 'helpful deeds' and 'acts of mercy' – and then conclude with a reference to 'teaching'.

Helpful Deeds

In my newspaper recently I read a wonderful story under the title 'The Chivalry Express'. It concerned a man who went to a railway station in London to have a quick cup of coffee. However, he spotted a young mother loaded down with luggage, pushing an 18-month-old son in a pram, and trying to hold the hand of his three-year-old brother. When no one else offered to help, the man went to her rescue, carried her bags for her, and stacked them carefully on board the train. However, as he turned to leave, the automatic doors slammed shut and the train left the station. The guard told the man that he was sorry but the next stop was York! The man therefore travelled to York, then back to London, a trip which he was made to pay for. At that point he felt the strain and said,

> I always like to help out if I can but this time I went too far. However, by Stevenage I was beginning to see the funny side.

The woman in question was effusive about her helper. She said,

> I am very grateful for his help and I was very embarrassed that he ended up so far away.

One of the gifts which Paul mentions is translated as the gift of 'helping'. In his list at the end of 1 Corinthians 12, he mentions *antilampseis*, a word which is not used anywhere else in the New Testament. This could be rendered as 'helpful deeds', and the gift itself could be defined as 'the special ability to help others who are in need'. Raymond Ortlund once described people with this particular gift as 'the glorious company of the stretcher bearers'.[5] He was referring to those in the story told in Mark 2:1-12 who brought their sick friend to be healed by Jesus:

> A few days later, when Jesus again entered Capernaum, the people heard that he had come home. So many gathered that there was no room left, not even outside the door, and he preached the word to them. Some men came, bringing to him a paralytic, carried by four of them. Since they could not get him to Jesus because of the crowd, they made an opening in the roof above Jesus and, after digging through it, lowered the mat the paralysed man was lying on.
>
> (Mark 2:1–4)

After that, Jesus forgives the man his sins, castigates the teachers of the Law for their cynical thoughts, and then tells the man to get up and walk, which he duly does, in full view of them all. The story ends with Mark reporting that everyone was amazed, and that the crowds praised God saying, 'We have never seen anything like this'.

I have heard many sermons on this passage, particularly by Charismatic preachers. In just about every instance, the story is used to illustrate the way in which Jesus operated in the spiritual gifts. Thus the following gifts are identified.

1. **Teaching.** Jesus is operating in the gift of teaching at the start of the story. This is the ability to preach the word with charismatic authority.

2. **Faith.** Jesus recognizes the faith of those who have brought the man for healing, and that the atmosphere is therefore conducive for a miracle.

3. **Prophecy.** Jesus sees that there is sin in the paralysed man's life, so he forgives him prior to performing the miracle.

4. **Discernment.** Jesus perceives the critical spirit within the teachers of the Law and exposes it.

5. **Healing.** Jesus heals the man, who gets up off his mat not only forgiven but able to walk.

In this kind of exposition, Jesus' use of the extraordinary gifts of the Spirit is revealed. However, it is a sobering fact that in all the sermons I have heard on this story, I can never remember hearing anyone applaud the stretcher bearers for their gift of *antilampseis*, 'helpful deeds'. Yet, if they had not been prepared to exercise that gift, the great healing event which followed would never have occurred. Few things reveal our predilection for the miraculous *charismata* more than this neglect of the gift of helping in the story in Mark 2. In our preference for the extraordinary and the sensational, we have completely forgotten the love, sweat and uninhibited desperation of those who helped the man to Jesus. This gift should therefore not be neglected in the Church. Indeed, the next time you attend a meeting where there is anointed worship, powerful teaching and wonderful demonstrations of the Spirit's power, ask yourself the following questions:

Who hired the venue?
Who put out the chairs?
Who set up the PA?
Who provided the notes?
Who arranged transport?
Who organized the coffee?
Who served the coffee?

The answer will be that it was an army of those with the gift of 'helping'; or, to use Ortlund's phrase, 'a glorious company of stretcher-bearers'.

The Gift of Mercy

Another neglected gift of service is the charism of mercy. Paul mentions this in Romans 12:8 when he writes,

Let the one who has mercy show it cheerfully.

This occurs in a list of *charismata* containing prophesying, serving, teaching, encouraging, contributing to the needs of others, and leadership. The gift itself is *ho heleon* in the Greek, best translated as 'acts of mercy'. So the particular anointing which we are studying here is 'the special ability to show acts of mercy to those in need, and to do that cheerfully'. James Dunn points out in *Jesus and the Spirit* that the adverb 'cheerfully' is the Greek word *hilaroteti*, from which we get 'hilarity'.[6] Though it may be dangerous to read our modern sense of the word into *hilaroteti*, it is tempting to adjust our definition of the gift and say,

The gift of mercy is the special, God-given ability to show acts of mercy to those in need, and to do it with unbridled joy and enthusiasm.

Thus, the charism of mercy is not a natural aptitude any more than speaking in tongues. Far from it! Paul knew that genuine mercy could not be summoned up in our own strength. He recognized

the impossibility of forcing ourselves to feel empathy with the plight
of the poor and needy. Rather, he understood that this special ability to feel compassion for the impoverished, the oppressed and the
marginalized was a gift of grace. For people with this particular
anointing, therefore, social concern is not a duty but a genuine
emotion. Practical compassion is supernaturally natural. As Peter
Wagner puts it:

> Every Christian is expected to be merciful. This is a role that reflects the
> fruit of the Spirit. But those with the gift of mercy make compassion
> and kindness their lifestyle. They do not simply react to emergencies, as
> every Christian is supposed to do. They continually seek opportunities
> to show pity for the miserable.[7]

It is often said of churches in the Charismatic Renewal that their
level of social concern is not what it should be. Critics of the
Renewal tend to focus on a lack of genuine, practical work amongst
the poor and those who are victims of injustice. They also point to a
lack of concern for ecology, and for the planet as a whole. Typical
amongst these is Jürgen Moltmann, who castigates Charismatics for
their lack of engagement with the world:

> We have to put a question to the 'charismatic movement': what about
> the *neglect* of charismata? Where are the charismata of the 'charismat-
> ics' in the every-day world, in the peace movement, in the movements
> for liberation, in the ecology movement? If charismata are not given
> us so that we can flee from this world into a world of religious dreams,
> if they are intended to witness to the liberating lordship of Christ in
> this world's conflicts, then the charismatic movement must not
> become a non-political religion, let alone a de-politicized one.[8]

There is some truth in this charge. However, critics like Moltmann
need to be careful not to overstate the case. The Pentecostal movement arose out of a revival at Asuza Street, Los Angeles in 1906,
and one of the striking features of this event was the way in which
the colour line was washed away in the blood of Christ. With the
coming of the Pentecostal fire, many of the social, racial and

economic divisions were broken down by the Holy Spirit. The same movement which recovered the *charismata* therefore spawned a radical commitment to the poor and an equally radical commitment to wipe out the evils of racism. As the Rev. Alexander Boddy wrote of Asuza Street:

> It was something very extraordinary, that white pastors from the South were eagerly prepared to go to Los Angeles to the Negroes, to have fellowship with them and to receive through their prayers and intercessions the blessings of the Spirit. And it was still more wonderful that these white pastors went back to the South and reported to the members of their congregations that they had been together with Negroes, that they had prayed in one Spirit and received the same blessings as they.[9]

Novatian once referred to the gifts of the Spirit as a necklace of jewels which adorns the Bride of Christ. Perhaps a *neglected* jewel in this necklace, at least in some Charismatic churches, is the gift of mercy. We have been more concerned to get saved and healed than to express God's love for the poor in constant acts of 'hilarious' mercy. We have been more concerned to minister to the spiritual and emotional needs of the middle classes than to feed the hungry and clothe the naked. I therefore have to agree with the sentiments of Ron Sider:

> Nothing excites me more than to hear stories of churches who are leading people to Christ and ministering to the needs of hurting people. I long for the day when every village, town and city has congregations of Christians so in love with Jesus Christ that they lead scores of people to accept him as personal Saviour and Lord every year – and so sensitive to the cry of the poor and oppressed that they work vigorously for justice, peace and freedom.[10]

Having said that, there are signs that an emphasis on ministering to the poor is becoming a more normative part of the mission of Charismatic churches. The two most charismatic Christians I know are an example of this. Their names are Paul and Jackie Ryalls, and they have been frequent visitors to our church. Four years ago they gave up their separate businesses, sold their £250,000 home, and responded to a call from the Lord to travel to Bosnia with aid for the hungry and the injured. Since that time they have made nineteen trips with a lorry of food, medicine and clothing gathered from the churches in their area. They have been shot at, abused and insulted. Yet the gift of mercy is so powerful in their lives that they have felt compelled by the love of God to keep going back, even when the likelihood of returning home safely looked very small. I know few people more charismatic in the Pauline sense than Paul and Jackie. They speak in tongues and they exercise 'mountain-moving faith'. They believe in the power of God to heal the sick and to deliver the demonized. Yet the overriding characteristic of their lives is 'mercy'. They have ministered mercy to those who have been shown mercy, and in the process they have constantly experienced God's mercy on one of the most dangerous mission fields in the world today. Paul and Jackie are a wonderful 'sign' of a growing integration between Charismatic Renewal and ministry to the poor. They are a living example of the beatitudes of Jesus:

> Blessed are the merciful, for they shall receive mercy.

The Gift of Teaching

The third and final gift which I feel bound to mention is the gift of teaching. This is also something of a neglected and under-valued charism in the Renewal today. Paul identifies this as a gift in Romans 12:7, where he says,

> If a person's gift is teaching (*ho didaskon*), let him teach.

This particular gift can be defined as the special ability to expound the Scriptures in an inspirational, dynamic and sound way. It is not the same as prophecy, as we observed in chapter 6. It is what James Dunn calls 'charismatic exegesis' – the anointed preaching of the Word of God for the edification of the Body of Christ.[11]

Another common criticism levelled against the Charismatic Renewal concerns its lack of emphasis on the Word of God. It is often said that there is a forgetfulness of Scripture in the Renewal, and this accusation is not unfounded. In the past there has been a popular, Charismatic view that there are two ways in which God speaks to us: through *logos* (the written Word) and *rhema* (the prophetic word). This view has led to a number of dangers, of which two seem immediately striking. The first is the fact that people have accepted this division at all. The truth of the matter is this: that the New Testament often uses *logos* where Charismatics would expect to find *rhema*, and it often uses *rhema* where they would expect to find *logos*. The very terms themselves are therefore dubious and misleading. Secondly, there has, at times, been a preference for *rhemata* (words of revelation), over *logoi* (the Scriptures). The extraordinary and miraculous nature of genuine prophetic utterances has led many to place this kind of revelation above that given in the Scriptures. This has, in turn, resulted in all kinds of problems, not least the gradual abandonment of the spiritual discipline of continuous Bible study in some contexts. Those who embrace this particular philosophy need to correct their views urgently. In contexts where this view is shared, the demise of Bible teaching is very visible. Instead of charismatic exposition of the Word of God, the Body of Christ is treated to a fast-food diet of passionate 'power narratives', i.e. testimonies of the dynamic ways in which God has used the preacher. Needless to say, all sorts of excesses ensue pretty quickly.

One of the gifts which needs to be reinstated is the gift of teaching. Indeed, the charism of teaching is the *missing* jewel in the necklace of the Bride of Christ. In some evangelical churches there is an emphasis on the spectacular charisms and a neglect of biblical preaching. In other evangelical churches there is an emphasis on biblical preaching but a total neglect of the gifts of the Spirit (particularly tongues, prophecy, healing and miracles). This sad polarization of the Word and the Spirit became particularly evident to me after I had written several articles for *Renewal* magazine on 'the Word and the Spirit'. Several months after they were published, a lady wrote the following letter to me:

I attend a conservative evangelical church where the teaching is moderately good. My own trouble is that I have no opportunity to exercise the gifts. I do not wish to rock the boat in our church (incidentally, I am a widow living alone). I have asked the Lord several times to let me go elsewhere, but his answer is always 'no'. How I long to see the power of the Holy Spirit displayed in our church.

I pass *Renewal* on to my daughter who attends a mildly charismatic church, but she feels the lack of teaching.

How I wish the two were united.

How I wish they were too! The truth is that the gift of teaching has, in the past, been somewhat neglected in Charismatic churches. The advent of the more miraculous *charismata* has distracted many pastors and leaders from two responsibilities: the responsibility of continuing to study and expound the Scriptures accurately and obediently, and the responsibility of identifying, training and releasing those in the Body of Christ who have nascent teaching abilities. As I have written elsewhere, this neglect of teaching is historically the main reason why times of renewal and revival are not sustained. However, I am encouraged by the fact that the Lord seems to be raising up a generation of young leaders who have a passionate desire to preach the Word in the power of the Spirit, and that many Charismatic networks are recognizing the need to set up conferences on 'The Word and the Spirit'. This is so vital because, as Spurgeon put it in his Dying Appeal, 'Men will not doubt God's Word when they feel his Spirit'.[12] So let the teachers come forth in the Renewal today and let there be churches where the Word is taught with demonstrations of the Spirit's power! (1 Corinthians 2:1–5).

The Blessing of the Gifts

The gifts of the Spirit, when embraced responsibly and in their totality, are an immeasurable gift to the Church. They are first of all a gift to the Church's worship of the Triune God. In this respect it is important to keep in mind the overall context of

Paul's teaching on the *charismata* in 1 Corinthians 12–14. These three chapters occur in a long section which is devoted to the Church's worship:

11:2–16	Order in Worship
11:17–34	Order in the Lord's Supper
12:1–31	Order in the Charismata
13:1–13	Order in Relationships (Love)
14:1–40	Order in the Use of Tongues/Prophecy

Indeed, the overriding theme of these chapters is summed up in 1 Corinthians 14:40: 'Everything [in the worship assembly] should be done in a fitting and orderly way.'

However, 'order' does not mean a suppression of the gifts of the Spirit in worship. It means a right use of the *charismata* for the upbuilding of the Church. When a church handles the gifts wisely and well, there is no doubt that its worship becomes alive in the Spirit. Where there was only form before, now there is fire as well. Where there was only structure before, now there is spontaneity as well. Where there was only liturgy before, now there is liberty as well. The blessing of the gifts in the context of public Christian worship is therefore considerable. No longer are people subjected to a controlled, cerebral and constrained form of worship. Now the emphasis is on a dynamic encounter with God in the immediacy of the Holy Spirit. God is no longer just the God of the far away but the God of the here and now. He is experienced in the power of the Holy Spirit, who is the immanent presence of the transcendent Lord. As the following account of 'charismatic worship' reveals, there is a world of difference between purely formal worship and worship in the Spirit:

In a back street in a working-class district we come to the sign of the 'Good News' ... Let us go in and find a place if we can. The room is almost always full. A hundred, two hundred, three hundred people? ... Most of those present come from the working-class district of Paris where we live: workmen and persons with small independent incomes, all together; equal numbers of men and women. There is a warm atmosphere of friendliness and fellowship. There is nothing which recalls the unbreakable ice of churches and chapels.

As newcomers, we were picked out and greeted (there is no reception committee). Someone hastened to give us a hymn book ...

One person speaks, but a hundred people vibrate in unison with his prophetic appeals. A wave of Hallelujahs and Amens, the expression of a spiritual whirlpool rising up from the very depths of faith ... almost convinces us that we are no longer in the twentieth century ... but have been carried back in time to Lystra, Pergamon, Antioch or Rome, amongst the early Christians ... The deacon makes an incisive call for immediate conversion. Some hands are raised. The sick are counted and invited to kneel in a semicircle on cushions around the platform. There they receive the laying on of hands ... There is silence for the message of those who speak in tongues. The interpreters are asked to translate.

Healing by anointing with oil or by laying on of hands; baptism in the Holy Spirit; *glossolalia* (speaking in tongues); a fervent expectation of the return of Christ. Nothing seems anachronistic to them ... With the joy of the newly converted, we step into the uncharted lands of the Acts of the Apostles. A breath of resurrection seems to blow across the pages of the First Epistle to the Corinthians, pages which, for so many Christians, remain a dead letter.[13]

What a beautiful description of charismatic worship! No wonder the French pastor who wrote these words said, 'it is sad to see how far all this is from normal Protestantism and its traditional worship'. The blessing of the gifts in relation to the Church's worship are immeasurable indeed. In a church where such gifts are combined with an emphasis on Bible teaching ('normal' Protestantism) and the sacraments ('normal' Catholicism), it is hard to imagine a form of worship more attractive, more engaging and more powerful.

So the *charismata*, stewarded wisely, are essential for worship. They are, secondly, essential for mission. There is no doubt that in New Testament times the extraordinary charisms were used in the context of preaching the Good News to the unconverted. Paul wrote that when he first came to Corinth he preached the message of the Crucified Messiah with demonstrations of the Spirit's power

(1 Corinthians 2:1–5). That this was his normal experience is confirmed by his words in Romans 15:18–20. There he writes of how he preached the Gospel of Christ 'by the power of signs and miracles, through the power of the Spirit'. Throughout the Acts of the Apostles, this combination of Scripture and the power of God is witnessed on just about every page. Even the writer to the Hebrews (whose letter has relatively little to say about the Holy Spirit) attests to this 'dunamistic' evangelism in the early Church.

> God also testified to it [the message of salvation] by signs, wonders and various miracles, and gifts of the Holy Spirit distributed according to his will (2:4).

There is therefore little doubt that many of the *charismata* which Paul describes in connection with worship are also available in the context of witnessing. This means that the New Testament encourages us to develop not only a charismatic ecclesiology but also a charismatic missiology. Indeed, it is a compelling fact that the Pentecostals and the neo-Pentecostals represent the fastest growing churches in the world, accounting for over a quarter of the Christians worldwide. The number of new believers being added daily – particularly in the context of poverty and persecution – is so massive that Pentecostalism is now identified as the fourth major movement in Christendom, alongside Roman Catholicism, Protestantism and the Orthodox Church. The evidence cannot therefore be denied: the gifts of the Spirit are a great blessing to mission as well as worship.

Come, Holy Spirit

So I want to end by asking us to dare to pray one of the oldest prayers of the Church, 'Come, Holy Spirit'. The churches today, particularly in Western Europe, are facing an almost unparalleled time of death and discouragement. Few people are attending acts of public Christian worship, yet many are hungry for an experience of God. The one obstacle that prevents most churches from opening their doors to the manifest presence of the Holy Spirit is simply pride. Most leaders, in my experience, have stifled this aspect of pneumatic presence because of theological presuppositions and personal fear. The major presupposition which prevents the 'coming of the Spirit' is the belief that the Spirit is already present in an act of worship. That is obviously true. However, while it may be right to say that the Spirit is present in a hidden way in such contexts, it is not true to say that he is present in a manifest way. Both forms of divine presence are necessary, however, and the path to having both is the bold and faithful prayer, 'Come, Holy Spirit'. Even a theologian as intellectually gifted as Thomas Aquinas recognized this fact. In his *Summa Theologiae*, he wrote:

> When Scripture speaks of the 'coming' of divine persons, it does not refer to a moving from absence into presence, since divine persons are always present, but a moving from one mode of presence into another mode of presence.[14]

Precisely. The mode of presence which is so desperately needed in the churches today is 'the manifest presence of God', and all this manifest presence becomes a reality when churches pray for *all* the gifts of the Spirit to be distributed in the fellowship.

> So Lord Jesus, let the Spirit come in power, and let the gifts be distributed in your Church. Help us to steward these gifts in a wise, loving and biblical way. Let the Church be always edified and let your name by always glorified. So come, Holy Spirit. Send the fire of Pentecost upon your Church. Revive your people, O Lord, and restore in our time the honour of your name.

Notes

INTRODUCTION

1   For an overview of recent scholarship, see my article, 'The Theology
    of Renewal and the Renewal of Theology', in the *Journal of
    Pentecostal Theology* (henceforth *JPT*), Issue 3, October 1993, pp.
    71–90. See also Mills, Watson E., *The Holy Spirit: A Bibliography*,
    Peabody, Hendrickson, 1988, for a comprehensive bibliography prior
    to 1987.

2   Du Plessis, David, *The Spirit Bade me Go*, Oakland, Du Plessis, 1963,
    p. 93.

3   Williams, Rodman, *Renewal Theology*, Vol. 2, Grand Rapids,
    Zondervan, 1990, p. 327.

4   Congar, Yves, *I Believe in the Holy Spirit*, Vol. 2, London, Geoffrey
    Chapman, 1983, p. 164.

5   Williams, Rodman, *Renewal Theology*, Vol. 2, p. 326.

6   For an excellent discussion of the relevance of 1 Corinthians
    13:8–10, see Ruthven, Jon, *On the Cessation of the Charismata*,
    Sheffield, Sheffield Academic Press, 1993, particularly chapter 3.

7   Schatzmann, Siegfried, *A Pauline Theology of Charismata*, Peabody,
    Hendrickson, 1989 edition, p. 78.

8   Quoted in Kydd, R., *Charismatic Gifts in the Early Church*, Peabody,
    Hendrickson, 1984, p. 44.

9   Hymn of the Great Vespers of Whit Sunday.

10 Congar, Yves, *I Believe in the Holy Spirit*, Vol. 2, p. 164.

I. THE WORD OF WISDOM

1 Wagner, Peter, *Your Spiritual Gifts Can Help Your Church Grow*, Eastbourne, Monarch, 1990 edition, p. 220.
2 Subritsky, Bill, *Receiving the Gifts of the Holy Spirit*, Chichester, Sovereign World Ltd, 1985, p. 32.
3 Petersen, Eugene, *The Message*, Colorado, NavPress, 1995 edition, pp. 403–4.
4 Watson, David, *Is Anyone There?*, London, Hodder & Stoughton, 1979, pp. 46–7.
5 Petersen, Eugene, *The Message*, p. 404.
6 Dunn, James E., *Jesus and The Spirit*, London, SCM Press, 1975, p. 79.
7 Cf. Robeck, Jnr, Cecil M., 'The Word of Wisdom', in *Dictionary of Pentecostal and Charismatic Movements* ed. Burgess, S. & McGee, G.B., Grand Rapids, Zondervan, 1988, pp. 890–2.
8 Quoted in Gaukroger, S. and Mercer, N., eds., *Frogs* 2, London, Scripture Union, 1993, p. 40.
9 Robeck, Cecil M., Jnr, 'The Word of Wisdom', p. 890.
10 Williams, Rodman, *Renewal Theology*, Vol. 2. pp. 352–3.
11 Edwards, J., *Jonathan Edwards on Revival*, Edinburgh, Banner of Truth, 1995 edition, p. 109.
12 Ibid., p. 115.

2. THE WORD OF KNOWLEDGE

1 Martin, Francis, 'The Word of Knowledge', in *Dictionary of Charismatic and Pentecostal Movements*, p. 528.
2 Pytches, David, *Come, Holy Spirit*, London, Hodder & Stoughton, 1995 edition, p. 93.
3 Subritsky, Bill, *Receiving the Gifts of the Holy Spirit*, p. 39.
4 Quoted in Pytches, David, *Come, Holy Spirit*, pp. 96–7.
5 Williams, Rodman, *Renewal Theology*, Vol. 2, p. 332.
6 Dunn, James E., *Jesus and the Spirit*, p. 219.
7 Rea, John, *The Holy Spirit in the Bible*, London, Marshall Pickering, 1990, p. 248.
8 See chapter 6, pp. 112–131.
9 Grudem, Wayne, *Systematic Theology*, Leicester, IVP, 1994, p. 1082.

10   In 1906, a great revival broke out at 312, Asuza Street, Los Angeles.
     This is commonly regarded as the birthplace of the Pentecostal
     movement.

11   Bartleman, Frank, *What Really Happened at Asuza Street?*,
     Northridge, Voice Christian Publications, 1962, p. 49.

12   Ibid., p. 76.

13   Ibid., p. 5.

14   Ibid., p. 55.

3. THE GIFT OF FAITH

1   Dunn, James E., *Jesus and the Spirit*, p. 211.

2   Quoted in Backhouse, Robert, ed., *1500 Illustrations for Preaching
    and Teaching*, London, Marshall Pickering, 1991, p. 338.

3   Frodsham, S.H., *Smith Wigglesworth. Apostle of Faith*, Springfield,
    Gospel Publishing House, 1990 edition, p. 156.

4   Ibid., p. 158.

5   Williams, Rodman, *Renewal Theology*, Vol. 2, p. 366. See also Smail,
    T., Walker, A. and Wright, N., ' "Revelation Knowledge" and
    Knowledge of Revelation: the Faith Movement and the Question of
    Heresy', in *JPT 5*, 1994, pp. 57–77. And also the classic exposé of
    the Faith heresy, McConnell, Dan, *A Different Gospel*, Peabody,
    Hendrickson, 1990.

6   Cf. Martin, Francis, 'The Gift of Faith', in *Dictionary of Charismatic
    and Pentecostal Movements*, p. 301.

7   Williams, Rodman, *Renewal Theology*, Vol. 2, pp. 364–5.

4. THE GIFTS OF HEALING

1   Williams, Rodman, *Renewal Theology*, Vol. 2, p. 368.

2   Dunn, James E., *Jesus and the Spirit*, p. 71.

3   Martin, Francis, 'The Gift of Healing', in *Dictionary of Charismatic
    and Pentecostal Movements*, p. 352.

4   Williams, Rodman, *Renewal Theology*, Vol. 2, p. 359.

5   Dunn, James E., *Jesus and the Spirit*, pp. 74–5.

6   Quoted in Grudem, Wayne, ed., *Are Miraculous Gifts for Today?*,
    Grand Rapids, Zondervan, 1996, pp. 213–14.

7   Deere, Jack, *Surprised by the Power of the Spirit*, Eastbourne,
    Kingsway, 1994, pp. 36–7.

8 Williams, Rodman, *Renewal Theology*, Vol. 2, pp. 392–3.
9 Buckley, Michael, *Christian Healing. A Catholic Approach to God's Healing Love*, London, Catholic Truth Society, 1990, pp. 18–19.
10 Ibid., p. 23.
11 This prayer was composed by Michael Buckley.

5. MIRACULOUS WORKS

1 Thigpen, Paul, 'Come, Holy Spirit! 2000 Years of Miracles'. First published in *Charisma* Magazine, September 1992.
2 Thigpen, Paul, ibid, p. 25.
3 Chavda, Mahesh, *Only Love Can Make a Miracle*, Eastbourne, Kingsway, 1990, p. 144.
4 Ibid., p. 137.
5 Ibid., p. 12
6 Ibid., p. 13.
7 McKay, John, 'When the Veil is Taken Away: The Impact of Prophetic Experience on Biblical Interpretation', in *JPT* 5, 1994, pp. 17–40.
8 Chavda, Mahesh, *Only Love Can Make a Miracle*, pp. 145–6.
9 Ibid., pp. 154–5.
10 Ibid., p. 151.
11 The best discussion concerning how to evaluate a miracle is in John Meier's *A Marginal Jew, Rethinking the Historical Jesus, Vol. II: Mentor, Message and Miracles*, New York, Doubleday, 1994. Chapter 17 is on 'Miracles and the Modern Mind' and contains a very even-handed approach to miracles. Meier's most helpful contribution is this: that he distinguishes between an historical judgement and a theological judgement concerning miracles. Historical criticism can take us only so far. After these more objective criteria have been satisfied (for which, see chapter 17), the investigator then has to make a theological judgement about whether the evidence points to a miracle.

6. THE GIFT OF PROPHECY

1 Dunn, James E., *Jesus and the Spirit*, p. 228.
2 Cartledge, Mark, 'Charismatic Prophecy: A Definition and Description', in *JPT* 5, 1994, pp. 79–120.

3   Grudem, Wayne, *Systematic Theology*, p. 1056.
4   Spurgeon, C.H., *The Autobiography of Charles H. Spurgeon*, London, Curts & Jennings, 1899, Vol. 2, pp. 226–7.
5   Williams, Rodman, *Renewal Theology*, Vol. 2, p. 387. The reader may also like to refer to David Aune's pioneering study, *Prophecy in Early Christianity and the Ancient Mediterranean World*, Grand Rapids, Michigan, Eerdmanns, 1983. He writes that 'the institution of Christian prophecy, it appears, does not readily lend itself to categorical conceptualization', and that 'Christian prophecy … did not possess a dominant form or structure' (p. 245).
6   Quoted in Cartledge, M., 'Charismatic Prophecy', pp. 112–3.
7   Grudem, Wayne, *Systematic Theology*, p. 1051.
8   Idem., p. 1058.
9   Idem., pp. 1056–7.
10   Idem., p. 1055.
11   Idem., p. 1056.
12   Fee, Gordon, *God's Empowering Presence*, Peabody, Hendrickson, 1994, p. 254.
13   Idem., p. 251.
14   *The Book of Margery Kempe*, trans. and with an introduction, by Tony Triggs, Tunbridge Wells, Burns & Oates, 1995, p. 184.
15   Dunn, James E., *Jesus and the Spirit*, p. 229.
16   Brueggemann, Walter, *The Prophetic Imagination*, London, SCM Press, 1992 edition, p. 13.

7. DISCERNINGS OF SPIRITS

1   Williams, Rodman, *Renewal Theology*, Vol. 2, p. 389.
2   Ibid., p. 394.
3   Hilton, Walter, *The Scale of Perfection*, Halcyon Backhouse ed., London, Hodder & Stoughton, 1992, p. 35.
4   Käsemann, Ernst, *A Commentary on Romans*, trans. Bromiley, G., London, SCM Press, 1980, p. 240.
5   Ibid., p. 241.
6   McQueen, Lawrence, *Joel and the Spirit. The Cry of a Prophetic Hermeneutic*, Sheffield, Sheffield Academic Press, 1995, p. 79. It is also interesting to note that the great revival theologian Charles Finney often encountered this kind of intercessory

groaning. His judgement on this particular phenomenon is well worth citing:

> I would sooner cut off my right hand than rebuke the spirit of prayer, as I have heard of its being done by saying: 'Do not let me hear any more groaning.'

Finney's view was that if leaders tried to stop this groaning in prayer, they would be resisting the Holy Spirit (*Finney on Revival*, E.E. Shelhamer, Bethany House Publishers, Minneapolis, Minnesota, 1980, p. 36).

7   Ibid., p. 80.

8   Ibid., p. 80.

9   Martin, Francis, 'The Gift of Discernment of Spirits', in *Dictionary of Charismatic and Pentecostal Movements*, p. 246.

8. KINDS OF TONGUES

1   Pain, Timothy, *Tongues and Explanations*, Eastbourne, Kingsway, 1986, p. 12.

2   V. Poythress, quoted in Turner, Max, 'Spiritual Gifts: Then and Now', in *Vox Evangelica* XV, 1985, pp. 43–4.

3   Spittler, Russell, 'Glossolalia', in *Dictionary of Charismatic and Pentecostal Movements*, p. 338.

4   The *Testament of Job* (c. 100 BC) is one of the Jewish writings excluded from the canon of Scripture. It is interesting because it sheds light on Jewish thinking between the end of the Old Testament and the beginning of the New. The *Testament of Job* is essentially Job's fictional, parting address to the children of his second wife. It concludes with an account of the heavenly songs sung by Job's three daughters as he ascends to heaven.

5   Pain, Timothy, *Tongues and Explanations*, p. 15.

6   Ibid., p. 27.

7   Martin, Ralph, *The Spirit and the Congregation*, Grand Rapids, Eerdmans, 1984, p. 9.

8   R. Spittler, 'Glossolalia', p. 336.

9   Cf. R. Spittler, pp. 336–7.

10 Cf. R. Spittler, p. 340.

11   Stibbe, Mark, *Explaining Baptism in the Holy Spirit*, Tonbridge, Sovereign World Ltd, 1995, pp. 19–26.

12   Grudem, Wayne, *Systematic Theology*, pp. 1076–7.

9. THE INTERPRETATION OF TONGUES

 1   Williams, Rodman, *Renewal Theology*, Vol. 2, p. 402.

 2   Pain, Timothy, *Tongues and Explanations*, p. 44.

 3   Parsin/Peres: *Peres* is the singular form of *Parsin*.

 4   Dunn, James E., *Jesus and the Spirit*, p. 244.

 5   Williams, Rodman, *Renewal Theology*, Vol. 2, p. 404.

 6   Spittler, Russell, 'The Gift of Interpretation of Tongues', in *Dictionary of Charismatic and Pentecostal Movements*, p. 469.

 7   Pain, Timothy, *Tongues and Explanations*, p. 19.

 8   Williams, Rodman, *Renewal Theology*, Vol. 2, p. 405.

 9   Ibid., pp. 405–6.

10   Dunn, James E., *Jesus and the Spirit*, p. 425.

11.   Williams, Rodman, *Renewal Theology*, Vol. 2, pp. 408–9.

CONCLUSION

 1   Schatzmann, Siegfried, *A Pauline Theology of Charismata*, p. 102.

 2   Welker, Michael, *God the Spirit*, Minneapolis, Fortress Press, 1994, p. 15.

 3   Ibid., p. 15.

 4   Gee, Donald, *Spiritual Gifts in the Work of the Ministry Today*, Springfield, Gospel Publishing House, 1963, p. 52.

 5   Wagner, Peter, *Your Spiritual Gifts Can Help Your Church Grow*, p. 224.

 6   Dunn, James E., *Jesus and the Spirit*, p. 250.

 7   Wagner, Peter, *Your Spiritual Gifts Can Help Your Church Grow*, p. 223.

 8   Moltmann, Jürgen, *The Spirit of Life*, trans. Kohl, M., London, SCM Press, 1992, p. 186.

 9   Quoted in Hollenweger, Walter, *The Pentecostals*, Peabody, Hendrickson, 1972, p. 24.

10   Sider, Ron, *Evangelism and Social Action*, London, Hodder & Stoughton, 1993, p. 16.

11 Dunn, James E., *Jesus and the Spirit*, p. 237.

12 Quoted in Bartleman, Frank, *What Really Happened at Asuza Street?*, p. 40.

13 Quoted in Hollenweger, Walter, *The Pentecostals*, pp. 459–60.

14 Thomas Aquinas, *Summa Theologiae*, quoted in Sullivan, F., *Charisms and Charismatic Renewal*, London, MacMillan, 1982, p. 70.

We want to hear from you. Please send your comments about this
book to us in care of zreview@zondervan.com. Thank you.

GRAND RAPIDS, MICHIGAN 49530 USA

WWW.ZONDERVAN.COM